WRIGHT PEAK ELEGY

WRIGHT PEAK ELEGY

A STORY OF COLD WAR NUCLEAR DETERRENCE, AND ULTIMATE SACRIFICE

ALAN D. MADDAUS

Epigraph Books
Rhinebeck, New York

Wright Peak Elegy: A Story of Cold War, Nuclear Deterrence, and Ultimate Sacrifice

Hardcover ISBN: 978-1-954744-73-8

Library of Congress Control Number: 2022907487

Book design by Colin Rolfe
Front and back cover photos by Nancie Battaglia

Epigraph Books
22 East Market Street, Suite 304
Rhinebeck, New York 12572
(845) 876-4861
epigraphps.com

CONTENTS

This book is dedicated to the memory of US Air Force B-47 crew members who perished in the line of duty supporting preservation of peace during the Cold War, and, in particular, Rodney Bloomgren, Kenneth Jensen, Albert Kandetski, and Melvin Spencer of Pete 67.

PREFACE TO THE SECOND EDITION

Distribution of the first edition and a successful book signing event at the Empire State Aerosciences Museum eventually led to input from an additional source: that while the content was accurate, there existed opportunities for clarification of key aspects of the story, as well as extension of it based on information generally not available to those lacking military aviation experience. An example of the former is a more precise and detailed explanation of the ill-fated Low Altitude Bombing System as implemented on the B-47; and of the latter an additional procedure put in place to greatly decrease probability of Controlled Flights into Terrain after the Wright Peak tragedy, particularly under low visibility conditions and in advance of availability of Terrain Avoidance Radar. The author is indebted to Frank Baehre, USAF Lt. Col. (retired), B-52 and FB-111 pilot and former curator of the Plattsburgh AFB Museum, for several communications sharing his knowledge of these and related subject matter.

Also added to the text is a poignant recollection from Neal Burdick, Adirondack editor/writer, of the effect the tragedy had on school children.

In addition, two iconic photos are included in this edition, one of a heavily loaded B-47 in take-off, with Assisted Take-Off Rockets activated and engines trailing black smoke at maximum thrust; and the other of the Me-262, the first jet powered aircraft in service.

Finally, Mike Collins, retired US Army aviator and pilot for New York State Aviation, suggested the following insight into the tragedy that ended the lives of brave and dedicated young airmen, with reference to the ancient proverb/poem describing a cascading series of failures leading to a disastrous final outcome, viz.,

> "For want of a nail, the shoe was lost.
> For want of a shoe, the horse was lost.
> For want of a horse, the rider was lost.
> For want of a rider, the battle was lost."
>
> Anon

The last line: "For the failure of battle the kingdom was lost—All for the want of a horse-shoe nail", doesn't apply here. Due to a combination of skillful diplomacy, building and maintaining alliances, the powerful deterrence represented by the USAF Strategic Air Command and sacrifices made by those who served, the Cold War ended.

FOREWORD

Whether related to an event in one's personal history—or a major event having impact on many people's lives—it is usually possible to look back and identify a logical starting point consisting of a place, circumstances, and a moment in time representing the very beginning.

In that context, the research project that became the basis for this book is more or less a result of my grandmother's parental guidance. When my father was a young man, ca. 1925, he aspired to become a forest ranger, and my grandmother wouldn't allow it due to concerns based on perceived dangers of that occupation. Similarly, she refused to assist him in getting a driver's license—so he drove without one for twenty years (understandably obeying all traffic laws and *never, ever* exceeding the speed limit). In the end, however, she prevailed on his choice of occupation.

He graduated from Columbia University with a BA in Mathematics, earned a master's degree there, finished coursework for a PhD at the University of Michigan in 1934, and completed his doctoral dissertation in absentia in 1940. His credentials for teaching mathematics substantially secured, in 1936 he became a *migrant college math instructor* over a seven-year period, taking in rapid succession math department positions at the Junior College of Patterson, New Jersey, (where he met and married mother); the Philadelphia College of Pharmacy and Science; and the Universities of Nevada, Oklahoma, and Oregon. During the last two years of World War II, he was employed by the US Army Air Corps (forerunner of the US Air Force) developing radar systems at MIT and then at the US Naval Research Laboratory in Washington, DC. Finally, in 1947 he took an assistant professorship position at Union College in Schenectady, New York—his days of wanderlust over—and in the rural village of Galway, New York, he and my mother raised four sons.

As soon as we were old enough, he indulged his previously constrained, latent interest and started hiking, taking us along. At first, lower summits like Pilot Knob (1,800-feet elevation) and Buck Mountain (2,330 ft.) east of Lake George, New York, then more strenuous climbs such as Snowy (3,898 ft.) and Mt. Marcy (5,344 ft.) in the Adirondacks, and Mt. Katahdin (5,269 ft.) in Maine's Baxter State Park. All of it left me with a sense of enjoyment in the activity of climbing higher and higher with increasingly expansive views of mountains, lakes and forests, and an associated sense of freedom from the normal constraints of life.

As I grew older, I stopped climbing for a period—college studies, summer employment, and then full-time employment reducing the amount of leisure time. My reacquaintance with the joys of climbing came my way by accident from a seemingly unrelated issue: an old house my wife and I had purchased with a badly leaking roof.

Short of funds to hire a roofing company to replace the roof, I contemplated replacing it myself. I mentioned this to a coworker, who offered to help. In exchange he asked that I accompany him on a climb of Mt. Marcy and Haystack in the Adirondacks. We quickly reached an agreement and over a two-week period removed and replaced 1,100 square feet of shingles, associated drip edge, and flashing material. Then on the afternoon of the agreed upon date in late September 1972, we got into his aging VW Karmann Ghia and drove up the Adirondack Northway to Keene Valley.

Parking at Keene Garden's lot, the location of a major trailhead to the High Peaks, we entered the woods at 4:00 p.m. and hiked in on rolling terrain with gear suitable for an overnight stay to a lean-to at Bushnell Falls. There we spent the night; the next morning we started up the trail for Slant Rock and Mt. Marcy beyond.

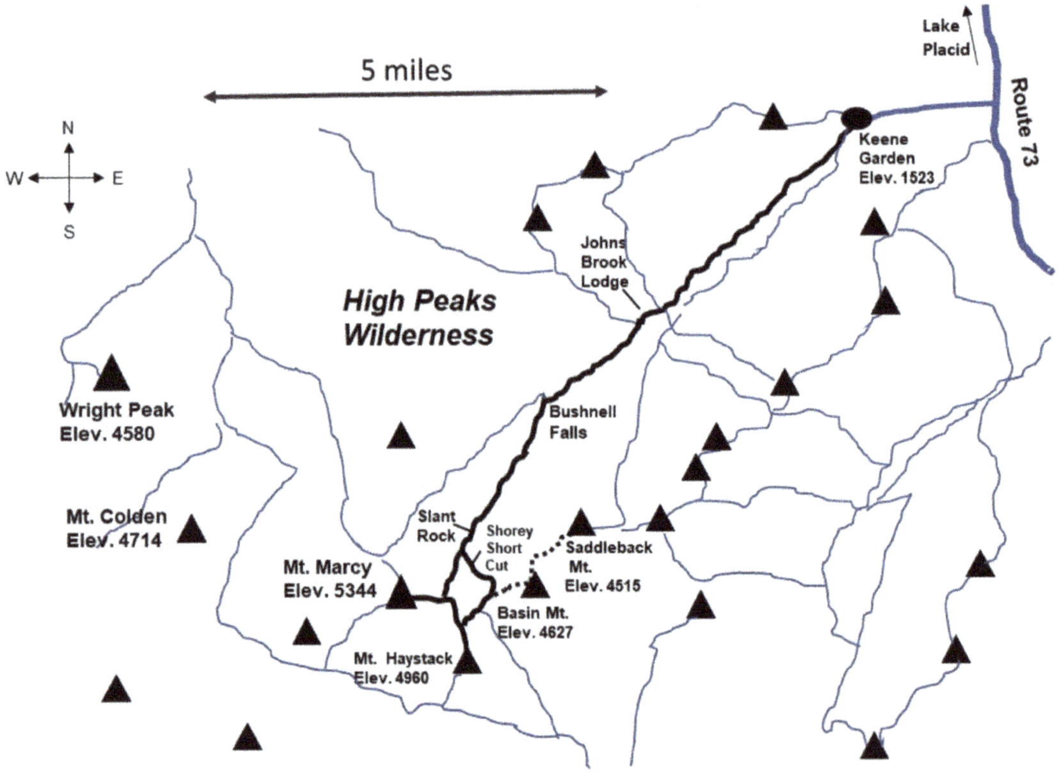

Map by Author.

My companion, who worked out daily with weights and running on a track, was in excellent physical condition—myself, not so much. At first, I tried to keep up, and then, as the trail steepened was reduced to taking fifty steps and stopping to catch my breath. I quickly lost sight of him. After about thirty minutes of struggling up the trail, I would see him in the distance, sitting on a boulder, smoking a Lucky. As I approached, he would stand up, stretch, and say, "man that felt good—now let's get going." And so it went until we reached the summit of Marcy.

After Marcy we retraced our steps to the branch trail to Haystack. Haystack was an easier climb, but when we finished that I was ready to go back to the car. My companion had other ideas, intent on adding the summits of Basin and Saddleback to the list for the day. Fortunately for me, he took a wrong turn, and we followed the Shorey Shortcut back to Slant Rock, thence to the Bushnell Falls lean-to. At that point I was completely exhausted, but a remedy existed.

At that time, black bears in the Adirondacks relied on town dumps for their food supply, thus minimizing their raids on "community" food stockpiled in the lean-tos. I took a cannister of sugar from a lean-to shelf, poured a cup into an empty coffee can, descended to the brook, and filled it with water (no worries about giardiasis, aka "Beaver Fever," at the time either—that would come later). After drinking the mixture my energy quickly returned, enabling me to hike the remaining two hours to the trailhead. My sugar high depleted, I fell asleep in the car, not waking up until we arrived home.

Following that experience, I resolved to get back in shape, using a dormant interest in running for cardio-vascular conditioning. Eventually I competed in road races and marathons at the local level and ran twice at Boston. With conditioning from running came the ability to traverse long sections of Adirondack trails and several summits in a single day. At one point I signed up for an Adirondack Mountain Club group hike in the Dix Range. The pace of the group didn't suit me, so I forged ahead leaving the group hours behind. For that indiscretion I was written up in a book published by one of the group members.[1] Lesson learned—as some members of guided parties during the 1996 Everest disaster would attest: *never hike with someone who is writing a book!*

It became apparent over time that with conditioning came the burden of not having hiking companions who could maintain a comfortable and enjoyable (for me) pace. My wife objected to me hiking trail-less peaks alone, so I repeatedly hiked in the well-traveled region bounded by Keene Valley and Heart Lake. This resulted in many climbs to the summits of Marcy, Haystack, Algonquin, and Wright.

As time went on, the story of a B-47 bomber crash on Wright Peak became more familiar. The first version I recall: a navigation error led the crew to believe they were over Rome, New York—elevation above sea level: 500 feet—rather than the much higher terrain of the High Peaks. While over the years I had climbed to the summit of Wright several times, I was generally in a hurry to traverse the MacIntyre ridge, descend to Lake Colden, and return to my car at Heart Lake through Avalanche pass—or over Mt. Colden—before nightfall.

Though I understood that wreckage of the aircraft was still visible near the summit, and a plaque had been installed in honor of the crew who had lost their lives, I did not take the time to explore. It all seemed a bit unreal—yes, unquestionably sad that men serving our country would perish in a crash. They were not able to eject, but why would an Air Force bomber be in that airspace and fly at that altitude? I discovered later that there were understandable reasons for both and that a crash of a B-47 was not a particularly unusual event.

One day I saw an article on climbing a slide on the east side of Wright, and there was mention of B-47 aircraft wreckage adjacent to it. A quick online search revealed a detailed description of a successful quest to find wreckage, in this case an almost full-length segment of a wing.[2] Another article contained a brief description of the circumstances connected with the tragedy. Catching my eye was the information that: "The plane had apparently veered about 30 miles off course on its return trip to Plattsburgh [from Watertown/Fort Drum] due to inclement weather and high winds and ventured into the high peaks . . ."[3] and that if it hadn't impacted Wright Peak it would have crashed on the northwest side of Mt. Marcy.

It just didn't make sense—the flight path from Watertown to Plattsburgh is east-northeast, and the path taken to impact Wright Peak was southeast—so the high winds forced an abrupt change in direction of 70 degrees? I'm not a pilot, but I do have some knowledge of aerodynamics, and a sharp turn due to action of wind seems implausible for a large aircraft traveling at 500 mph. Equipment failure, possibly an aileron control problem may have been the cause, or more likely, the fateful turn was due to deliberate action by the crew. That's how this project began.

* * * * *

In a similar vein, the 1962 Wright Peak tragedy had its roots in actions taken by the Allies as an outcome of World War II, well before its end, became clear. Final accommodations made to the Communist government of the Soviet Union at the Yalta Conference in February 1945 related to occupied territory control, combined with the rapid spread of communism and threat of world domination led to a need for strategic deterrence by the United States based on a capability for rapid delivery of nuclear bombs.

Fulfilling this need was a newly developed jet engine bomber which held the promise of an unstoppable attack. The first jet bomber was a prototype for most commercial and military jet-powered aircraft to follow but suffered from shortcomings in technology and reliability that only operating experience could fully define. Shortcomings aside, to fulfill its promise new and demanding tactics were developed that eventually proved successful but required continuous training under all manner of flight conditions, including zero visibility and severe weather over mountainous terrain. Hence aircrews took risks that would be unthinkable in today's environment, and some, including the crewmen aboard a B-47 bomber—call sign "Pete 67"—paid the ultimate price. This is their story in the context of world and national events of that period.

In telling it I am aware of General Curtis LeMay's remark: "In my opinion, first person accounts . . . are historically more reliable than most historian's accounts."[4] With that in mind, I have used sources associated with the events to the greatest extent possible.

NOTES: FOREWORD

[1] James R. Burnside, *Exploring the Adirondack High Peaks* (Schenectady, NY: High Peaks Press, 1996), 310, 313–314.

[2] Kevin "Mudrat" MacKenzie, "Wright Peak Airplane (aka) Wright Slides," Videos from the Top Forum, (photo set and text), copyright 2014, posted July 27, 2014 (last edited October 5, 2015), www.vftt.org/forums/showthread.php?56957-Wright- Peak-B-47-Wing-Wreckage-Right-Left-Wing-and-new-Angel-Slides (vftt.org).

[3] New York State's Adirondack Mountains (adirondack-park.net), "An Air Force Bomber Crashes into Wright Peak," based on a compilation of Jamestown, NY *The Post-Journal* issues compiled by Kristi Davis, page added March 11, 2000, www.adirondack-park.net/history/b47.wright.html.

[4] Mark Natola, ed., *Boeing B-47 Stratojet—True Stories of the Cold War in the Air* (Atglen, PA: Schiffer Publishing, 2002), 7.

View of Lake Placid, NY and Whiteface Mountain from Wright Peak. ©Nancie Battaglia 2021.

INTRODUCTION

When hiking in the Adirondack High Peaks, a part of the forever-wild region of the six-million-acre, or 9,375-square-mile (thinking of it as a square area one hundred miles on a side, one won't be far off) Adirondack Park, the sights and sounds of civilization occasionally intrude. This is noteworthy near some trailheads—where the noise of vehicles on highways is present—and at the summits where

Avalanche Pass, Adirondack Mountains. ©Nancie Battaglia 2021.

highways, settlements, and small cities are visible. For example, from the summit of Algonquin, second highest peak of the forty-six above 4,000 feet altitude and a strenuous climb, there is a clear view of the village of Lake Placid with the Olympic ski jumps in the foreground.

Single-engine plane over Wright Peak, Mt. Marcy in background © Nancie Battaglia 2009

Civilization is also evident through the sights and sounds of aircraft in flight over the region. Most of the aircraft are small and single-engine, some equipped with floats for landing on lakes and ponds. Occasionally one will see a business jet flying at low level into the airport at Lake Placid. The orientation of Avalanche Pass is such that it is on a path for landing there, and in one memorable instance I watched as such an aircraft flew below me as I stood on the summit of Mt. Colden. Looking down, I could see the pilot in the forward part of the cabin. I waved and imagined that he dipped his wing in response, though it might have just been for course correction.

Abandoned small plane wreckage souvenir. Photo by Author.

Business jet in Avalanche Pass on approach to Lake Placid Airport. Photo by Author.

Other signs of aircraft use over the High Peaks can be seen in jet trails high in the sky, faint sounds of engines, and on occasion the signature sound sequence made by a military jet that has broken the sound barrier—a plane streaking across the sky in silence; then a loud boom followed by engine noise, indicating that the shock wave generated by supersonic flight had passed by. And finally, there is the wreckage of planes that have crashed there—fifty in all over the years, according to Scott van Laer, Adirondack Aviation Archeologist.[1] Most of them off the beaten path but occasionally evident in debris carried out of the woods to a frequently traveled area and then discarded, as if the individual who had found it had lost interest.

Undoubtedly the most famous and accessible of the crash sites is that of a Boeing B-47 US Air Force bomber from the former Plattsburgh Air Force Base that collided with Wright Peak near the summit during the early morning of January 16, 1962, killing all four crew members. Growing up in the Adirondack foothills 100 miles from the location of that tragedy, I have no distinct recollection of the event, nor for that matter, the importance of the B-47 bomber fleet to the security of our nation during the height of the Cold War.

By contrast, closer to the scene, the impact of the tragedy on children my age was understandably devastating – to wit:

> "When I walked into Mr. Arcarese's sixth grade classroom at SUNY Plattsburgh's Campus School that cool, grey morning I was brought to a halt by the eerie silence. Some of my classmates wore downcast expressions. Mr. Arcarese, normally a jovial guy, appeared somber. No one spoke. No one made eye contact.
>
> "As I recall, I took my seat and asked the girl in the next row, who lived on the Plattsburgh Air Force Base, what was going on. She told me a plane stationed at the base, and its crew, were missing.
>
> "The date was January 16, 1962, a Tuesday. I was 13 days shy of my 12th birthday. I remember all of it vividly."[2]

But as a child I developed an interest in assembling aircraft models from kits and then hanging them for display on a wire that was stretched across my bedroom, near the ceiling. The centerpiece of that display was a B-47 model—long and sleek with six pylon-supported jet engines under "shoulder mounted" swept-back wings—that was unlike anything I had ever seen. Even to me, unaware of the importance of that aircraft—militarily or as the prototype for current commercial jet aircraft—it stood out as something special, making the B-24 bomber of World War II fame hanging next to it look like a strange out-of-place antique.

And special it was, designed in response to the nuclear threat represented by the hostility of the Soviet Union and its interest in world domination. The nuclear-armed B-47 program was a credible deterrent, keeping that nation at bay for more than a decade through the Cuban Missile crisis. But not

Boeing B-47 Stratojet. USDOE – Wikimedia Commons

Consolidated B-24 Liberator. USAF – Wikimedia Commons

without numerous crashes and a distressing cost in lives of the brave men who flew them. So, while the crash in the Adirondacks may have appeared to the uninformed as a singular event, it was very unfortunately part of the routine.

NOTES: INTRODUCTION

[1] Rick Karlin, "Aviation archaeologist searches for long-lost planes in Adirondacks," *Times Union* (Albany, NY), November 3, 2015.

[2] Neal Burdick, Anatomy of a plane crash – Review of Wright Peak Elegy by Alan Maddaus, Special to the Adirondack Daily Enterprise, September 15, 2022. With a modification, in communication with the author, December 16, 2023.

CHAPTER 1

COLD WAR, NUCLEAR DETERRENCE, AND THE ADVENT OF JET BOMBERS

Arising out of mistrust between the US, Western Europe, and the Soviet Union, the Cold War had its roots in the outcome of World War II and unresolved issues from the Yalta Conference of February 1945, which was attended by President Franklin D. Roosevelt, Great Britain Prime Minister Winston Churchill, and the Soviet Union's leader, Josef Stalin. In exchange for a Soviet commitment to participate in an expected invasion of Japan, Roosevelt and Churchill acquiesced to Soviet demands for determining the post- war political destinies of the countries involved in the war.

Quickly, the Eastern European countries of Czechoslovakia, Bulgaria, Romania, Hungary, and Poland fell under Soviet control; despite an agreement with Stalin that the governments would be determined through a democratic process, communists seized power. This led to Winston Churchill's famous reference to the "Iron Curtain"—but more importantly, a fear on the part of the free world that the goal of the Soviet Union was world domination through country-by-country communist takeovers.

And so it happened: In February of 1946, Stalin made a speech in which he declared that communism and capitalism were incompatible. This was followed in February 1948 by the communist takeover

Top: British Prime Minister Winston Churchill, U.S. President Franklin Roosevelt, and Soviet General Secretary Joseph Stalin meet at Yalta. February 1945. Photo by US Government Employee. Wikipedia.

of Czechoslovakia, the blockading of Berlin from land travel through East Germany, communist control of China (1949), and Soviet support of North Korea's invasion of South Korea (1950). During the same time frame, Russia tested its first nuclear weapon and began development of advanced delivery systems, which was ample reason for the US and Western European Allies to focus on means of countering a Soviet Attack.

In a review of US military defense strategy—"The Air Force and Strategic Deterrence 1951–1960" by George F. Lemmer, a declassified Department of Energy document—the author writes:

> As a result, the United States reversed its long-standing policies and began building a large, permanent, and expensive military establishment. The principal threat came from the Soviet Union. In addition to its formidable land armies, which confronted the exhausted countries of western Europe, Moscow had acquired atomic weapons with which it might strike the United States itself. To ward off such a calamitous event, the nation might have chosen to appease the Russians and return to its traditional isolationism or to launch a preventive war. Instead of these extremes, it decided to seek security through containment of the Soviet Union and preventing Communist aggression. This middle approach demanded skillful diplomacy, large-scale rearmament, economic and military aid to allies, and collective security arrangements such as the North Atlantic Treaty Organization (NATO).
>
> Militarily the United States adopted the concept of strategic nuclear deterrence. This required a peacetime military effort much greater than had ever been attempted before plus continuing innovations of new strategic programs to meet changes in the military threat. The goal of deterrence, of course, was to discourage potentially aggressive states from taking steps that might bring on a new world war. Its success depended upon the clear communication of U.S. intentions to the Soviet Union and on the size and nature of American military forces. By the late 1950s the cost of these forces had stabilized at about $40 billon—approximately 10 percent of the gross national product. This investment supported strategic deterrence, continental defense, and some elements for limited wars. Through most of the 1950s the U.S. emphasis was on building up the bomber and missile forces of the Strategic Air Command (SAC). The military policy of strategic deterrence appears to have succeeded. Although the cold war remained grim, the Soviet Union was very careful to avoid actions which might lead to a direct military confrontation with the United States and a third world war.[1]
>
> It was not until the early 1950s that the Air Force was provided the resources to expand and modernize its strategic bomber forces. Prior to this time the strategic force consisted of World War II B-29s, the B-50 (an improved version of the B-29), and the B-36, which entered combat units in 1948 and provided the range that air leaders had been dreaming about for a generation. Then in late 1951 the first all-jet B-47s arrived. These six-engine, medium

bombers had about the same combat radius as the B-29 but in every other respect exceeded the performance of the other bombers.[2]

Development of jet bombers by the US began in 1943 when military planners concluded that the jet engine would result in bombers fast enough to greatly mitigate the defense effectiveness of enemy fighter aircraft while having operational range competitive with the then-current piston-engine-driven aircraft—the underlying motivation for the assessment: continued mauling of US bombers in raids on Germany by German fighters.

Frank Whittle of Great Britain received a patent for the turbojet (jet engine) in 1932. In 1935, Hans von Ohain started work on a similar design in Germany, and it is often claimed that he was unaware of Whittle's work, though he later confirmed he had knowledge.[3] A major problem with both designs was the use of a centrifugal compressor with inherently large diameter and therefore excessive drag-inducing frontal area that made adaptation to aircraft propulsion questionable.

Small, Swift, and Sinister, the German Luffwaffe Messerschmidt Me 262 Schwalbe (Swallow) Photo by US Air Force, National Museum of US Air Force

Ansel Franz, a Junkers Motoren (Jumo) turbocharger design engineer from Austria, who held a doctorate from the Technical University of Berlin, solved this problem by replacing the centrifugal compressor with an axial flow compressor section,[4] providing the same performance characteristics with a diameter similar to that of piston engines. The reduction in diameter came about through increasing the length of the compressor while simultaneously reducing the diameter—"streamlined" low-drag-inducing shapes inherently long and slender rather than short and wide. The Jumo-004 engine design was completed

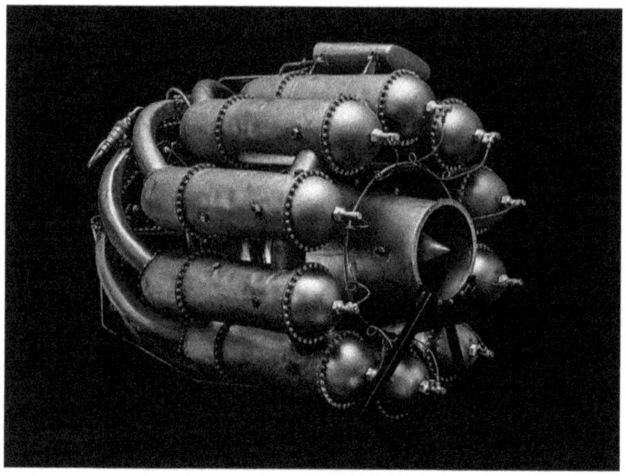

Whittle Jet Engine—National Air and Space Museum. Photo by Dane A. Penland, Wikimedia Commons.

in 1939, a test run in October of 1940 and the first flight in a German Messerschmitt Me 262 military aircraft in July of 1942.[5] Mass production of this engine was delayed until 1944, due to vibration and fatigue problems. Thus, its impact on the outcome of the war was minimal. However, by all accounts it was a successful design, and represented a formidable adversary for Allied piston-engined fighters, e.g. the P51 Mustang, having significantly higher top speed, though lesser maneuverability. But too few found their way into combat and at a very late period of the war. Nevertheless, it was the first use of a jet engine in military (or commercial) service.[6]

The source of US military planners' information on favorable prospects for jet engine applications to military aircraft was Great Britain, development proceeding in parallel with the German effort. Much of the initial information came from a meeting and communications with the British Technical and Scientific Mission, a.k.a. the Tizard Mission, named after Henry Tizard, chairman of the Aeronautical Research Committee.[7]

The Mission visited the United States in September of 1940 with the intent of securing agreement to use US capabilities for development and production of advanced military hardware and technology related to items on a diverse list, including: radar, gunsights, explosives (including the atomic bomb), and Frank Whittle's jet engine.

At a meeting with Vannevar Bush and George W. Lewis of the US National Defense Research Committee (NDRC) Tizard reportedly conveyed the intensity of the British work to develop the jet engine, without providing any details. Later Bush would realize that a similar US NACA [National Advisory Committee for Aeronautics] project was far behind, advising General Henry "Hap" Arnold, commander of the US Army Air Force, that the British were planning for production in five months. Bush's recommendation was the US make arrangements for producing the Whittle engine by a company with required capabilities.[8] As a manufacturer of turbochargers for military aircraft, including the B-29 bomber, GE was the natural choice.

Following a visit to Great Britain in July of 1941, where General Arnold observed demonstrations of a prototype jet engine airplane, he arranged for a Whittle jet engine produced by Power Jets to be shipped to the US along with plans for a more advanced and powerful engine.[9]

In October of 1941, a complete Whittle engine along with drawings were flown to Boston and transported to the GE Lynn, Massachusetts, plant, where a team of ultimately one thousand had been assembled to work on the project. The schedule was tight—the GE team had committed to building the prototype and having it ready for test in six months. A separate building was devoted to the project, and fewer than twenty individuals understood what they were working on. The initial prototype, the General Electric 1A, was essentially based on the Whittle W.2B/23. It first ran on April 18, 1942 and developed a static thrust of 1,250 pounds.[10] In October 1942 an upgraded version of this engine, the GE I-16 (a.k.a. J31—the Air Force designation), producing 1,600 pounds of thrust, powered the Bell P-59A on an initial test flight at Edwards Air Force Base.[11] Two years later an uprated J31 design, produced 4,000 pounds of thrust.[12]

The next generation of GE jet engines began with introduction of the J35, which incorporated an axial compressor developed in cooperation with the NACA, and was followed by the J47 (initially, 5,000 pounds of thrust) which became the world's most produced jet engine as well as the engine selected for the B-47.[13]

General Electric J-47 Jet Engine. National Museum of the USAF/USAF Photo.

With jet engine development well underway, in 1945 the application effort to military aircraft took an interesting turn. In April of that year American armed forces accompanied by British Troops were advancing through Germany. On April 11 the Americans liberated the Nazi concentration camp of Buchenwald. The following day they reached the German town of Voldenrode, home of the Luftfahrtforschungsanstalt (Aeronautical Research Institute), a secret facility for airframe, aircraft engine, and aircraft weapons testing. A week later American scientists, aerodynamicists, and engineers of the 125th Liaison Squadron arrived on a mission ordered by General Arnold to investigate the technology under development there. Included in the small group were noted aerodynamicists Hugh Dryden and Theodore von Kármán, but most importantly, as it would turn out, Boeing aerodynamicist George Schairer.

Schairer reviewed the German aerodynamics research program, facilities, and data; his handwritten report to a colleague at Boeing went into detail on the Pfeilfluge (arrow wing), more commonly referred to as the "swept wing." This innovation, one simply put as an attachment of the wings to the fuselage at an angle of approximately 30 degrees from perpendicular, had been explored theoretically by other aerodynamicists, including Robert Jones of the NACA, but evidently without the level of detail of the researchers at German ARI or the benefit of wind-tunnel testing. The ARI critical findings were: a) that sweeping of the wings increased the "critical Mach Number," or in simpler terms the speed at which a sharp increase in aerodynamic drag occurs, enabling a higher maximum speed for a fixed level of engine power [i.e., a faster aircraft]; and b) that anything [which in practical terms means engines] attached to the wing leading edge along the span from fuselage to wing tip would adversely affect this benefit.

In essence, these two requirements dictate the wing geometry for most jet aircraft, commercial and military, in service today: the wings are swept and the jet engines, unlike their piston-engine predecessors embedded in the wing surface, are supported by struts or pylons below the wing.

Aware of his responsibility as an agent of the US government to share the swept-wing revelation with aerodynamicists employed by other companies, Schairer instructed his Boeing colleague to make the information available for unrestricted competitor use. In the end, however, it was Boeing that implemented the first successful prototype design. Boeing held the advantages of an engineering management team that focused on incorporating cutting-edge technology in new designs and an exceptionally large and powerful wind tunnel adjacent to its engineering offices that was ideally suited for test evaluation of concepts like the swept wing.[14]

> *Author's Note: The following is a very much condensed description of the events that ensued in the development of the Boeing's B-47 Stratojet Bomber, drawn from the detailed accounts in references cited in chapter endnote 14.*

Work on the next generation bomber at Boeing had begun in October 1943 in response to a USAAF request for proposal (RFP) for "design of an experimental airplane using one or more TG-180 (J35) jet engines." Based on initial Boeing studies, a speed of 600 mph with fuel consumption competitive with piston engines was deemed possible. For reference purposes, the primary USAAF bomber of that era was the B-29, which had a top speed of about 350 mph.

The initial Boeing *conceptual design* had a conventional straight-wing geometry and was essentially a B-29 with 4 jet engines, two each in "nacelles" (streamlined housings) blended into the wing leading edges. It lost in competition to entries from Republic and Hughes. However, the Army Air Force Material Command encouraged Boeing to continue its research. Boeing subsequently went through four design iterations, the last of which deviated from the B-29 configuration in that the four jet engines were mounted adjacent to the wing-fuselage attachment just behind the cockpit. At that point, in December 1944, contracts were awarded to five competing aircraft manufacturers. But the USAAF Engineering Division remained unimpressed with the Boeing submissions.

All that would slowly but steadily change due to the swept-wing revelations of George Shairer. In September 1945, Boeing resubmitted their proposal based on a swept-wing design and increasing the number of jet engines from four to six, but with the engines still mounted in the top of the fuselage. The Air Force rejected the design but encouraged Boeing to continue wind tunnel research to "solve problems associated with high-speed jet bombardment aircraft."

Finally, there was a breakthrough—subsequent research and wind tunnel testing resulted in a thin cross-section, swept-wing design with jet engines mounted on struts or pylons below the wing, three on each wing, two inboard in a single nacelle, and the third engine outboard near the wing tip. This was declared by the USAAF Engineering Division as a "step beyond current bombers, . . ." and a Boeing proposal for two prototypes was accepted.

Following some modifications to the conceptual design associated with landing gear arrangement, wing area and seating arrangement—the first B-47, the XB-47, was rolled out in September 1947 to "considerable enthusiasm from the military and the press." It was clear that a new era in aircraft design had arrived. One member of the press described the aircraft as looking like a "torpedo on a roller skate with wings added as an after-thought," an interesting interpretation of a design viewed as negative at the time.

Flight testing began in late October 1947 under the exceptionally capable leadership of Robert Robbins, an MIT aeronautical engineering graduate with eight years of test pilot experience. After months of preliminary tests, including one in which a J47 jet engine was installed on the underside of a B-29 and (in flight) the engine was started and evaluated for response, the time for the first flight of the XB-47 arrived. Observing an abundance of caution, a runway was selected so the flight path would avoid heavily populated areas, and the crew was prepared to fire eighteen ATOs (assisted take-off rockets) attached to the rear fuselage to gain sufficient altitude for ejecting if serious control or engine problems occurred.

Robbins mentioned this to his wife (eight months pregnant with their son) in attempt to calm her down prior to the first flight after his unfortunate demonstration of how flexible the wings were during a walk around of the plane. He had taken hold of a wing tip and forced it up and down ten inches. She was understandably horrified. The first takeoff was from the Boeing field in Seattle before a group of Boeing personnel involved with design and manufacturing of the prototype. Some admitted later that they were concerned that the plane would not lift off. The event was marred by a false engine fire indicator light on the initial takeoff run, but there was success on the second attempt, and the plane made the initial flight to the Moses Lake Air Force facility, 170 miles east, with no significant difficulties.

Following the successful test program Air Force interest in the B-47 was sidetracked, a situation reflecting a faction of Boeing's business leadership team's assessment that the company's economic future was aligned with the B-50, a traditional propeller/piston engine design. However, Boeing President William Allen understood that the Air Force "preferred a future powered by jet engine," and at a crucial meeting with the Air Force Material Command Leadership including General Kenneth Wolfe, Allen forcefully prevailed on the General to take a flight in the B-47. One flight was all it took; the next day a commitment was made for an order eventually finalized to include 65 aircraft. Before production ended in February 1957 the USAF would take delivery on 2,042 B-47 aircraft, the majority of which were bombers. They were distributed on twenty-five bases in the United States and seventeen overseas bases in close proximity to the Soviet Union.

The 1955 Paramount Picture film "Strategic Air Command" with James Stewart and June Allyson contains aerial photography of the B-47 and provides visual insight on the dramatic appearance of the B-47 during takeoffs and in-flight, including refueling and landing.

NOTES, CHAPTER 1

1 George F. Lemmer, "The Air Force and Strategic Deterrence 1951–1960," USAF Historical Division Liaison Office, December 1967,1–2. https://nsarchive2.gwu.edu/nukevault/ebb249/doc09.pdf.

2 Ibid.,15–16.

3 Hans von Ohain: Wikipedia, https://en.wikipedia.org/wiki/Hans__von__Ohain.

4 Walter J. Boyne, ed., *Air Warfare: An International Encyclopedia: A-L* (Santa Barbara, CA: ABC-CLIO Publishing, 2002), 234.

5 Ibid.

6 Messerschmitt Me 262: https://wikipedia.org/wiki/Messerschmidt__Me__262

7 Tizard Mission: Wikipedia, https://en.wikipedia.org/wiki/Tizard Mission.

8 Ibid.

9 Ibid.

10 "Blast from the Past: The Story of GE's First Jet Engine," https://www.youtube.com/watch?v=C__gkYasLH20.

11 General Electric J31: Wikipedia, https://wikiwand.com/en/General__Electric__J31.

12 Aviation History—GE Aviation, https://geaviation.com/company/aviation-history.

13 General Electric J-47, Wikipedia, https://en.wikipedia.org/wiki/General__Electric__j47.

14 Mark Natola, ed., *Boeing B-47 Stratojet—True Stories of the Cold War in the Air* (Atglen, PA: Schiffer Publishing, 2002), 8–14; C. Mike Habermehl and Robert S. Hopkins III, *Boeing B-47 Stratojet: Strategic Air Command's Transitional Bomber* (Manchester, UK: Crecy Publishing, 2018), 11–24.

Boeing B-47E—1956. Photo by USAF, Wikimedia Commons.

Boeing 737-600—1998. Photo by Adrian Pingstone, Wikimedia Commons.

CHAPTER 2

ATTRITION AND THE TRANSITIONAL JET BOMBER

There were many versions of the B-47 bomber, starting with the XB prototype, followed by "models" A, B, and E, as well as configurations intended for reconnaissance and for electronic counter measures. By far the highest number produced was the E, accounting for 1,341 planes of the 2,042 total. Specifications for the E, compared with a recent commercial jet aircraft, are listed below.

The two aircraft are similar in swept-wing design, overall dimensions, cruising speed, range, ceiling, and engine thrust. There are major differences aside from military versus commercial use in: number of engines, maximum take-off weight and distance, and fuel load—not to mention the sleek appearance of the B-47 in contrast to the bulk of the 737.

	B-47E[1]	Boeing 737-600[2]
Introduction Date	January 1953	September 1998
Crew	3	6
Passengers	1	149
Armament	2 – 20mm tail cannons	
Bomb Load (lbs.)	25,000	

Similarities		
Overall Dimensions		
-Length (feet)	107	102
-Wingspan (feet)	116	112
-Height (feet)	28	41
Cruising Speed (mph)	500	520
Range (miles)	4,035	5,200
Thrust (lbs. total)	35,820*	39,000**
Ceiling (feet)	40,500	41,000
Differences		
Engines	6 – Model J47-25 (GE)	2 - Model CFM-56-7 (GE-Snecma)
Weight (lbs. @ takeoff)	230,000	153,499
Take-off Distance (feet)	10,400	6,200
Fuel Load (gallons)	16,318	6,878

Notes:

**At maximum takeoff weight, thrust was 43,200 pounds with water/alcohol injection, and up to thirty-three ATO rockets could be installed for additional thrust.*

***Manufacturers maximum thrust rating.*

"Pride of the Adirondacks" B-47E Tail Guns. ©Nancie Battaglia 2021.

The much longer takeoff distance of the B-47 is generally attributed to the low efficiency of early jet engines at low speed combined with aircraft weight at maximum fuel load. The large difference in fuel load for significantly shorter range is, again, an engine efficiency issue.

The B-47 was referred to as a medium bomber, fast and capable of carrying a large load of nuclear bombs, making it intimidating and deadly to adversaries. The absence of defensive weapons in locations other than the tail was testimony to its ability to outrun enemy fighter aircraft of the period.

That is not to say it was the perfect weapon-delivery solution for nuclear deterrence. The problems were at least threefold: basic shortcomings in the design, a requirement for a high level of skill and attention by the pilots, and reliability of systems. Shortcomings in the design included, but were not limited to:

Loaded for Bear: The rocket-assisted take-off of a Boeing B-47B, powered by GE J47 engines and Solid Rocket Thrusters [aka ATOs], engines injected with water-methanol for thrust augmentation producing black smoke. 15th of April 1954. Photo by US Air Force, National Museum of US Air Force.

1. Insufficient Range—The combat radius, the maximum distance a military aircraft can travel and return without refueling, was 2,000 miles. "Maligned as the perfect bomber should war break out with Canada or Mexico, the B-47 was limited by its poor range."[3] For reference purposes the distance from Loring AFB, Limestone, Maine, to Moscow (Russia) is approximately 4,200 miles; so hypothetically, if war were declared, it would need to be refueled twice to get there and return. Not that it was impossible; aerial refueling had been developed and the first air transfer to a B-47 had taken place in January of 1951.[4] But it was an edgy situation because piston engine tankers like the KC-97 were so slow that the B-47 had to fly on the verge of stall during the process. Later, the introduction of the jet-powered KC-135 greatly mitigated that problem, but B-47s still crashed due to loss of control during refueling.

The other solution was to make use of overseas bases in countries of Allies like Great Britain, and in Europe and Northern Africa. A drawback to that was the exposure of these countries to attack by the Soviet Union and concerns about the safety of nuclear weapons on their soil.

2. Sluggish Jet Engine Performance—Jet engine technology was in its infancy when the requirements of the B-47 were defined. There is no question that the GE company, with government support (NACA for example), responded well in developing an engine that would provide sufficient thrust to meet the maximum speed requirement of 600 mph. The principal problem was sluggish throttle response—fifteen or more seconds from idle to full throttle,[5] which put the pilot in a difficult situation if there was a sudden need for power (for example, to abort a landing). Power for takeoffs was also lower than optimum, requiring the use of ATO (Assisted Take Off) rockets and water/alcohol injection for thrust augmentation. When the aircraft was heavily loaded, up to thirty-three individual rockets attached to the underside of fuselage near the tail section were fired simultaneously, providing approximately ten seconds of increased thrust. The effect was visually dramatic; the problem: if the takeoff needed to be aborted, it was exceedingly difficult to address. *There was no way to shut the rockets down.*

3. High Landing Speeds—The aerodynamically clean, low-drag airplane design, combined with positive engine thrust even at idle, resulted in very high-speed landings. When combined with poor braking effectiveness and the need for the unique "bicycle arrangement" of the landing gear—front and back wheels on the fuselage mounted at the underside centerline with lateral support from outrigger wheels (similar to bicycle training wheels) attached to the underside of the wings, which required very precise touchdowns—it was a prescription for loss of control during landings.[6] The fix was to provide drag chutes—one that was deployed before landing to require a higher engine thrust setting during an approach to help with sluggish engine response time if a go-around was required[7] and one to augment the action of the brakes after touchdown.

4. Narrow Range of Stability at Cruise Conditions—At high altitudes and cruising speed the aircraft would enter an instability region aptly called the "*coffin corner*"[8] where the boundaries of the high- and low-speed stall regions converged. Hence, pulling the nose up to maintain altitude would result in a slight loss in airspeed and entrance into a region of low-speed stall. Correcting for this by adjusting the nose downward would increase the airspeed slightly and cause the approach to a region of high-speed stall. Stall, being synonymous with loss of control, was therefore to be avoided. This was manageable for an experienced pilot, but might consume all his attention, and if another problem arose the result could be disastrous.

There were additional issues, some of which the crews learned to live with, and others, like wing failures during flight that required a massive and urgent program to correct. Due to these problems the B-47 earned a reputation as a very demanding plane to fly. A selected quote from a pilot, more measured than some others, is illustrative in this regard: "'It was just simply an airplane you couldn't fool with.[9] You had to be with it all the time. When you treated it right, if you were very careful with it, if you didn't push it beyond its envelope, it was a delightful plane to fly.[10] It could bite you in a minute.'"[11]

Another pilot, less reserved in providing his perspective, opined: "'I didn't love the B-47. I considered it an adversary that would have killed me if I had given it the chance.'"[12]

On the positive side, reflecting the powerful deterrent that the nuclear armed B-47 represented: "'Throughout the 1950s, the B-47 served as the lynch pin of America's strategic defense.[13] With the serious threat of nuclear conflict hanging over the world, the Strategic Air Command's massive fleet of 1,500 B-47s presented the Soviets with a retaliatory threat they could neither match nor contain.'"[14]

But bite it did—as clearly reflected by "attrition" records. *Attrition*, generally used to describe the process of defeating an opponent by causing continuous losses in personnel, equipment, and supplies resulting in a loss of will to fight, is applied here euphemistically in reference to aircraft losses of the B-47 program.[15] From its onset in 1950 to the last military flight at the end of 1967, there was a continuous, distressing accumulation of accidents which generally resulted in either total destruction or write-offs of aircraft and crewmen loss of life. A detailed graphical representation of the B-47 attrition records is provided below, by year:

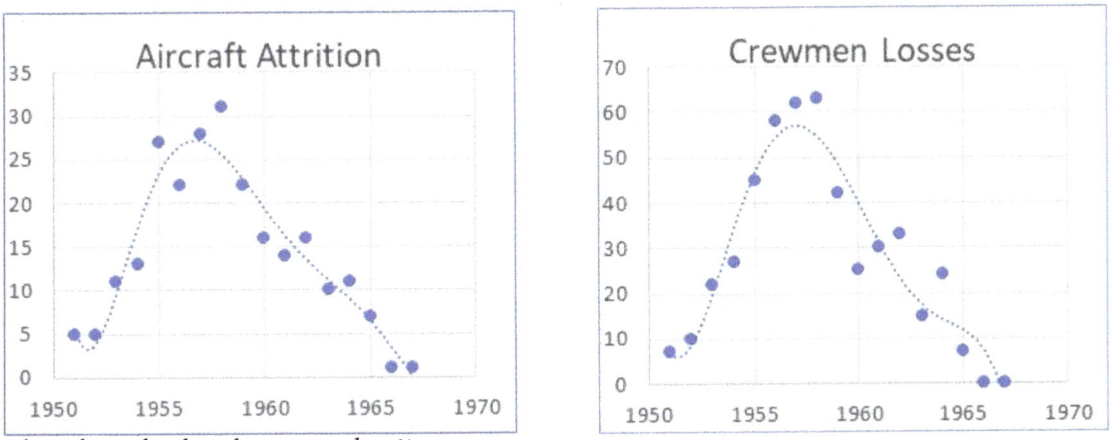

Charts by author based on source data.[14]

(One takeaway from the above: for every crash, two out of the three or four crew members on the aircraft perished.)

By comparison, these losses far exceed those of the B-52 program and would be unacceptable by today's standards. The tilt-rotor Osprey Vertical Takeoff and Landing aircraft is a case is point; while there is a lot of current concern about its safety record, it is far better than that of the B-47. That the B-47's safety record was tolerated can be attributed to the depth of concern related to Soviet miltary power and the persception that without the threat of massive B-47 nuclear weapon delivery, war was a certainty.

The accidents occurred on the ground and during takeoffs, landing, flight and inflight-refueling, and training manuevers. They involved on-board fires and explosions; engine, radio and navigation, control and control surface, and canopy failures; structural failures including wing and fuselage separations;

pilot error, incapacitation, and fatigue; weather conditions including poor visibility, turbulence, and cross winds; and unknown factors. There were collisions with other aircraft including tankers during air-fueling, fighter jets, and other B-47s both in the air and on the ground; and collisions with terrain in the context of Controlled Flight into Terrain (CFIT). Over the seventeen-year period of operation, based on analysis of accident data contained in *Boeing B-47 Stratojet: Strategic Air Command's Transitional Bomber*,[16] 205 B-47s (10% of the fleet) were totally destroyed in crashes, resulting in 477 crewmen deaths and 25 deaths of civilians. This is reasonably close to an independent assessment: 203 lost in crashes and 464 deaths (the latter may not include civilians).[17]

Details of accidents are documented by Habermehl and Hopkins in *Boeing B-47 Stratojet: Strategic Air Command's Transitional Bomber* as well as other sources, presumably all having a basis in Official USAF Accident Reports. Some are eerily brief and chilling. Examples:

> June 21, 1954—"Fuel vapors ignited in the bomb bay of a B-47E from Hunter AFB, Georgia during the flight, producing a series of explosions causing the airplane to crash.... All four crewmembers on board were killed."[18]
>
> April 6, 1956—A B-47E explodes and bursts into flames at 2000 feet altitude 15 minutes after departing from Lincoln AFB, Nebraska. The crew of four was killed. The cause of the crash was never determined.[19]
>
> February 5, 1958 A B-47E assigned to March AFB, California, disappeared fifty miles West Southwest of San Miguel Island on a low altitude practice bomb tossing mission. No trace was found. The crew of three perished.[20]
>
> July 27, 1964—"The [B-47E assigned to Lincoln AFB] failed to accelerate during takeoff and crashed, killing the crew of four."[21]

There are also stories of heroic actions taken by the aircraft commanders or crewmembers to land a damaged aircraft and save lives: A noteworthy example described under the title, "The Man in the Burning Bomber,"[22] recounts actions taken by a copilot to successfully land a flaming B-47 with a missing canopy rather than bail out—after the other crewmembers had successfully done so—and leave an incapacitated observer onboard to face certain death.

The events that almost ended the B-47 program as the lynchpin of US Nuclear Deterrance occurred in 1958. The B-47 was originally designed to provide high-altitude weapons delivery to the target in support of the SAC plan to strike targets deep in the Soviet Union should war be imminent. By the mid-1950s it became apparent that the increasing effectiveness of detecting high-altitude aircraft by radar, combined with the development of surface to air missiles (such as the US Nike),[23] higher-speed jet fighters (F-100 capable of supersonic level flight)[24] and the concern that the Soviet Union had similar capabilities, made that tactic obsolete. Consequently, there was a shift in SAC tactical approach to low-level, high-speed attack in 1956[25] as a means of avoiding detection. This shift resulted in a "bomb

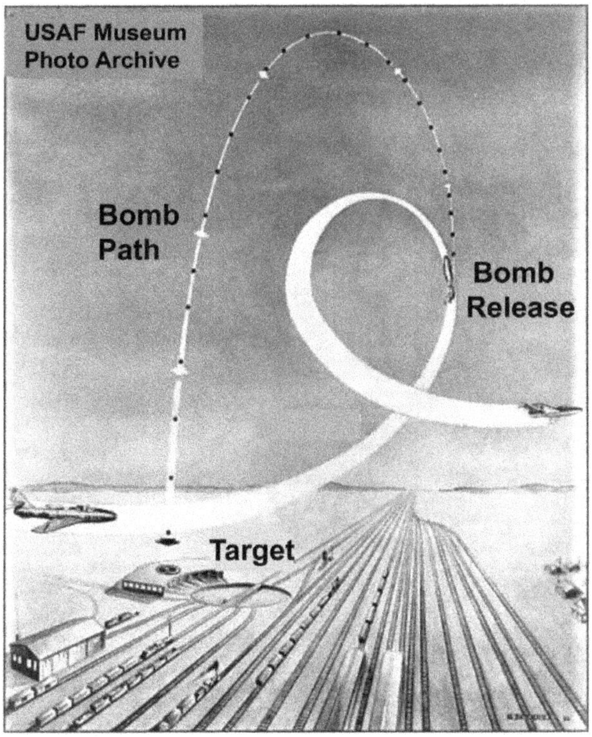

LABS procedure, USAF. Image: Wikimedia Commons

tossing" maneuver known as LABS (Low Altitude Bombing System).

The LABS procedure was based on low-altitude, high-speed penetration of enemy airspace. Approaching the target, the aircraft would engage in a bomb tossing maneuver starting with a sharp vertical climb. At the near vertical position the bomb would be released and follow an upward trajectory before falling on the target as shown in the LABS diagram. In the meantime the aircraft would continue in the Immelmann profile [of the above figure, a maneuver named after Max Immelmann, German WW I ace pilot] through to inverted flight. The B-47 LABS did the half-loop, but then continuing until the nose was about 20 to 30 degrees nose-low so it was going "downhill" and gaining airspeed before executing the half-roll back to right-side-up. That put extra distance as the aircraft continued to descend and accelerate away from the impending blast [of the nuclear bomb].[26] The problem: The B-47 was not designed to withstand the high wing and fuselage loads imposed by the manuever. First publicly demonstated at Eglin Air Force Base in Florida on May 7, 1957,[27] it became the standard procedure for low-level bombing until a series of crashes associated with failures of the wings occurred. In March and April 1958, there were five related accidents, the first of which occurred when a B-47 making an ATO takeoff at Homestead Air Force Base broke into four parts, resulting in the deaths of the four crewmembers. That was followed the next day by an instance in which a wing broke off in flight. Then in rapid succession, three more similar accidents occurred, resulting in destruction of the airplanes and deaths of all onboard in a span of not much more than a month.[28]

The root cause of the problem was determined to be fatigue cracks in and around critical bolt holes in the wings along with failure of the bolts—including a large one shaped like a milk bottle that held the wing to the fuselage. Addressing this critical issue, a total of 1,142 arircraft were modified and repaired in the Milk Bottle Program.[29]

Given that the B-47 was the primary deterrent against outbreak of a nuclear war with the Soviet Union, the Air Force had a daunting task of managing bad news, as it would clearly give the enemy reason to believe the military position of the US was weaker than anticipated. In response to public concern about the growing list of accidents, the Air Force issued a one-sentence statement to the *New York Times*: "The Air Force said today it was making a 'thorough investigation' of recent B-47 jet bomber accidents but did not consider the ratio of accidents to flying time 'excessive or alarming. . . .'"[30]—while at the same time launching a massive all-out emergency program to understand the root causes and repair and strengthen the affected wing and fuselage components. Largely successful, the fleet was restored to service, albeit with some lingering safety concerns, until the B-52 Bomber and ICBMs could take its place.

In the meantime, a modified approach to the Low Altitude Bombing System was adopted.

NOTES, CHAPTER 2:

1 Joseph F. Baugher, *Joe Baugher's Encyclopedia,* "USAAC/USAAF/USAF Bomber, Aircraft: Third Series," (blog), June 7, 2008,

USAAC/USAAF/USAF Bomber Aircraft-Third Series (joebaugher.com).

[2] Modern Airliners: Boeing 737 Specs, (blog), Modern Airliners.com,

https//:modernairliners.com/boeing-737/boeing-737-specifications/Boeing 737 Specs - Modern Airliners.

[3] C. Mike Habermehl and Robert S. Hopkins III, *Boeing B-47 Stratojet: Strategic Air Command's Transitional Bomber* (Manchester, UK: Crecy Publishing, 2018), 9.

[4] Ibid., 41.

[5] Mark Natola, ed., *Boeing B-47 Stratojet—True Stories of the Cold War in the Air* (Atglen, PA: Schiffer Publishing, 2002), 12.

[6] Ibid.

[7] Frank Baehre, in communication with the author, December 4, 2023.

[8] Habermehl and Hopkins, *Boeing B-47—SAC's Transitional Bomber,* 275.

[9] Natola, *Boeing B-47—True Stories*, 15; Habermehl and Hopkins, Boeing B-47—*SAC's Transitional Bomber*, 276.

[10] Ibid.

[11] Ibid.

[12] Ibid.

[13] Ibid.

[14] Natola, *Boeing B-47—True Stories* 15.

[15] Habermehl and Hopkins, *Boeing B-47—SAC's Transitional Bomber,* 274–301.

[16] Ibid.

[17] Walter J. Boyle, "The B-47's Deadly Dominance," *Airforce Magazine*, February 1, 2013, .0213dominance.pdf (airforcemag.com)

[18] Habermehl and Hopkins, *Boeing B-47—SAC's Transitional Bomber,* 291.

[19] List of accidents and incidents involving military aircraft (1955–1959). Wikiwand, April 6, 1956.

[20] Ibid.

[21] Habermehl and Hopkins, *Boeing B-47—SAC's Transitional Bomber,* 298.

[22] Natola, *Boeing B-47—True Stories*, 60–64.

[23] Chris Adams, *Inside the Cold War: A Cold Warrior's Reflections* (Maxwell Air Force Base, AL: Air University Press, 1999), 8.

[24] Laurence K. Loftin Jr., "Early Jet Fighters: Through the Transonic Range," (part 2, chapter 11), in *Quest for Performance: The Evolution of Modern Aircraft*, NASA History Office/NASA Scientific and Technical Information Branch, www.history.nasa.gov/SP-468/Contents.htm.

[25] Habermehl and Hopkins, *Boeing B-47—SAC's Transitional Bomber,* 55.

[26] Frank Baehre, in communication with the author, December 4, 2023.

[27] Wikipedia: Toss Bombing, Toss bombing - Wikipedia

[28] Habermehl and Hopkins, *Boeing B-47—SAC's Transitional Bomber,* 55.

[29] Ibid., 59.

[30] H. *Bruce Franklin, "Broken Bombers—How the U.S. Military Covered Up Fatal Flaws in the B-47 Stratojet with Disastrous Results," Military History Now (blog), September 16, 2018,* Broken Bombers – How the U.S. Military Covered Up Fatal Flaws in the B-47 Stratojet with Disastrous Results - MilitaryHistoryNow.com

CHAPTER 3

GENERAL CURTIS LEMAY: FLEXIBLE TACTICS AND THE IMPORTANCE OF TRAINING

At its best, the B-47 was an impressive aircraft—smooth, nimble, and fast—capable of delivering nuclear bombs by avoiding, tactically diminishing, or overwhelming Soviet defenses but at a price measured in loss of aircraft and, more importantly, crewmen lives. One could argue that the XB-47 would have better served simply as the conceptual design for the B-52, which remains today's heavy bomber, rather than a prototype for a 2,000-aircraft B-47 fleet. The problem was that in 1948 there was not time available to develop the B-52 to meet the immediate need. To quote Donald Rumsfeld, Secretary of Defense under President George W. Bush, at a much later date addressing a complaint that the National Guard was being sent to Iraq with antiquated equipment: "You go to war with the army you have, not the army you might want or wish to have at a later time."[1] (Incidentally, that statement, however factual, was understandably not well received.)

And although the Cold War was not one of battles, innumerable deaths, and massive destruction, the threat of a nuclear apocalypse made it close enough. School children of that era can easily remember

Top: General Curtis LeMay, Chief of Staff, United States Air Force. Photo by USAF, Wikimedia Commons.

"duck and cover" drills—crawling under desks and covering their heads as protection (!) against the effects of a nuclear blast.

The Commanding General of the US Strategic Air Command, Lieutenant General Curtis LeMay, reluctantly accepted the reality of the situation, but reportedly never stopped complaining about it—responding to upgrade plans to address the latest B-47 flaw with "'How deep do we have to bury this thing before you dumb SOBs stop digging it up.'" LeMay "hated the Boeing B-47 Stratojet."[2] While the timing of his remarks is not provided, it may well have been during the LABS crisis. His preference was the B-36, a slower aircraft, but one with at least twice the range. In addition to range limitations, the B-47 had significant production difficulties and was viewed as a fair-weather bomber. It was a dangerous aircraft to fly due to its sluggish engines and tendency to be unstable and uncontrollable outside of a narrow range of flight conditions; *bad weather just added to the problem.*

> <u>*Author's Note:*</u> *the following is largely a condensed version of the Curtis LeMay story as presented in* LeMay—The Life and Wars of General Curtis LeMay[3] *with several contributions from other sources.*

General Curtis LeMay's personality had wildly conflicting attributes; his behavior has been characterized as cold, blunt, harsh, socially inept, and at times self-destructive. His lack of concern about killing enemy civilians is well documented. "'I'll tell you what war is about,' he once told Sam Cohen, the inventor of the neutron bomb, 'You've got to kill people and when you kill enough of them they stop fighting.'"[4] LeMay developed and implemented the plan for fire-bombing Japanese cities during the latter part of World War II—in one night one hundred thousand civilians were killed and fifteen square miles of Tokyo were burned to the ground. His justification: "You simply can't fight a war without some civilian casualties. . . . We didn't start this war but the quicker we finish it the more lives will be saved and not just American. We want to avoid killing civilians if possible but keep in mind that the Japanese workers who manufacture weapons are part and parcel of their military machine. My first duty is to protect and save as many of our crews as possible."[5]

Robert McNamara, a one-time subordinate and eventually LeMay's boss as Secretary of Defense in the Kennedy administration said of him, related to high abort rates of bomber missions during WWII: "One of the commanders was Curtis LeMay—Colonel in command of a B-24 [*sic*, actually a B-17] group. He was the finest combat commander of any service I came across in war. But he was extraordinarily belligerent, many thought brutal. He got the report. He issued an order. He said, 'I will be in the lead plane on every mission. Any plane that takes off will go over the target, or the crew will be court-martialed.' The abort rate dropped overnight. Now that's the kind of commander he was."[6]

And while he showed little compassion for aircrews whose preference was to avoid flying through heavy flak, (it is hard to blame them) regardless of the strength of defenses his plane flew over the target and dropped the bombs. His approach was to channel anxiety into anger; at mission takeoffs "according to one copilot who flew with him: 'He bites down on his cigar and manages to turn from anxious to angry in just a few seconds He turned his fear into fury. Iron-Ass his men called him, but never to his face.'"[7]

Later, as Air Force Chief of Staff, during a critical moment in our nation's history, he clearly demonstrated a tendency toward self-destructive tactlessness. LeMay, highly critical of President Kennedy's response to the Cuban Missile crisis, said to Kennedy: "You're in a pretty bad fix, Mr. President." Kennedy's reply: "You're in there with me—personally."[8] LeMay's stature was presumably diminished when President Kennedy was successful in negotiations to defuse the crisis with Soviet leader Khrushchev.

But it is also clear he cared deeply about his wife and daughter, individuals on his leadership team, and the men who served under him, the latter reflected in that he would not ask them to do anything that he would not participate in. His willingness to fly the lead bomber in attacks on heavily defended German industrial targets was famously acknowledged by President Kennedy, with whom he had an uneasy relationship, in remarks following the Cuban Missile Crisis. "'If you have to go,' [to war] John Kennedy once said, [possibly with a mischievous grin on his face, since LeMay was no longer a combat mission participant] 'you want LeMay in the lead bomber. But you never want LeMay deciding whether or not you have to go,'"[9]

Curtis Emerson LeMay was born in Columbus, Ohio, on November 15, 1906, to parents of limited means; his father was a migrant worker who never held a job for more than a few months, his mother was a domestic servant. From the time he saw his first airplane at the age of four he had one dream—flying. During his childhood years he worked after school to help support his family, building businesses including one that distributed newspapers—at the expense of engaging in sports or dating. He enrolled in Civil Engineering at Ohio State and joined ROTC, a path to the limited number of slots in the Army Air Corps, working nights at a foundry to pay his way. At the age of twenty-one he joined the National Guard to improve his Air Corps chances. He commissioned as a Second Lieutenant Field Artillery, and after what seemed like an interminable wait, he sent a telegram to the War Department in Washington, DC explaining his desire, and in due course was authorized to enlist in the Air Corps.

At the time (1927) there were no US plans for engaging in war; the two oceans were seen as buffers from potential enemies. However, far-sighted individuals in the Air Corps—Billy Mitchell (of 1942 Tokyo Raid WWII Fame), Henry "Hap" Arnold (Commanding General of the Army Air Force 1942–1946), and Carl Spaatz (Commander, US Strategic Air Forces in Europe 1944)—shared a strong belief in airplanes as a means of breaking the stalemate of trench warfare.

Curtis LeMay graduated from Advanced Flight School in October 1929, having gained recognition as a gifted pilot. In the period prior to preparations for World War II he engaged in training and public relations exercises (air shows) while he honed his piloting and leadership skills and became an exceptional aircraft navigator. In 1934 he was promoted to First Lieutenant. When he had the opportunity to drop his first bomb, he gained an appreciation for the skill required to hit the target and transferred from fighters to bombers.

B-17 Flying Fortress Photo by USAF. Wikimedia Commons.

In 1937 the War Department woke up to the military build-up in Japan and Germany. The B-17 Bomber developed by Boeing was available for use and became a vehicle for sending a message of US Military strength. Named the Flying Fortress in recognition of the thirteen machine guns located at nine locations on the fuselage, it had a range of 3,750 miles, maximum speed of 300 mph, maximum bomb load of 10,000 pounds and a crew of twelve.

War in Europe broke out in September 1939 with the Nazi Germany invasion of Poland. LeMay, a Captain, was immediately engaged in ferrying supplies to Great Britain. Recognized as the top pilot in the Air Corps, now the US Army Air Force, he was promoted to Major.

Following the December 7, 1941 attack by Japan at Pearl Harbor, LeMay was sent to the West Coast to lead defense against an attack on the mainland. The stunning defeat of the Japanese fleet at Midway provided relief from that possibility, and at the end of October 1942 he was on his way to Europe as commander of a squadron of B-17s.

Colonel Curtis LeMay officially congratulates a bomber crew of the 306th Bomb Group in front of their B-17 Flying Fortress. Photo by US Government Employee, Wikimedia Commons. B-17.

There he showed his abilities as a leader and expert tactician. Tactics for bombing of heavily defended German industrial centers were based on zigzag maneuvering and ten seconds over the targeted area at night. The unfortunate outcome was that very few bombs hit the target, while at the same time the bombers were mauled by German fighters and antiaircraft fire. LeMay determined that by tightening up the formations to make maximum use of the B-17 Flying Fortress machine gun defenses and shifting the bombing runs to daytime with one long straight run over the target, much better results could be obtained. And to demonstrate convincingly that he believed in the approach, he piloted the lead bomber. The cost remained high; many aircraft were lost, and airmen killed or wounded principally by flak; planes returned to England with dead and dying men aboard. But the bombs hit their targets and the US and Great Britain started winning the war of attrition.

Colonel LeMay was promoted to Brigadier General in 1943 and Major General in March 1944. Transferred to India in 1944 to lead B-29 operations there, he was quickly reassigned to lead operations attacking Japan.

B-29 Stratofortress. Photo by USAF, Wikimedia Commons.

The B-29 Stratofortress represented an advancement in capability relative to the B-17 and B-24 bombers, having a maximum speed of 350 mph, a maximum bomb load of 20,000 pounds and five remote controlled gun turrets, in addition to one in the tail section.

Here LeMay's expertise in tactics again resulted in a change in approach. Due to cloud cover and variability of winds over Japan, high-altitude daytime target bombing had achieved poor results. LeMay studied the problem and concluded that the alternative of low altitude, massive nighttime raids with incendiary bombs would be more effective, particularly given that the structures in Japan's cities were predominantly wooden. The first raid, on March 9, 1945, involved three long lines of bombers in staggered rows at low altitude, the first entering the target area dropping bombs to mark front and back of the zone, the remainder saturating the zone with incendiaries. Individual clusters of thirty eight bombs containing napalm and phosphorous were set to explode at 2,000 feet; 1665 tons of bombs were delivered to the target area in Tokyo in a single night.[10]

The results were catastrophic for the civilian population—one hundred thousand people died, mostly by asphyxiation; the resulting fires destroyed fifteen square miles of the city and a million people were left homeless.

More Japanese cities were firebombed, Nagoya, Osaka, Kobe, Nagoya a second time; then bombing was suspended for a time when stockpiled Napalm had been used up.

General LeMay was labeled a "blood-thirsty maniac"[11] by Radio Tokyo. Discussions of the morality of massive civilian casualties were held behind closed doors in Washington. LeMay defended the action, pointing out that the quicker the war was ended, the better for all concerned, and avoiding an invasion of Japan to end it would prevent the loss of many more American lives—up to a million, according to one estimate.

Firebombing continued into August as a race evolved to see if it would make use of the atom bomb unnecessary. The "physics experiment in the desert" proved successful on July 16, 1945. LeMay thought it would be safer to send one bomber loaded with the weapon, rather have a fleet surrounding it, as single weather and observation planes routinely flew over Japan without opposition. An atomic bomb was detonated over Hiroshima on August 6, delivered in a bomb-tossing maneuver by the B-29 *Enola Gay*; eighty thousand people died instantly, followed by sixty thousand later by radiation poisoning. In the absence of a response from Tokyo, firebombing continued. The second atomic bomb was dropped on Nagasaki on August 9. Firebombing continued. Finally, the Japanese surrendered on August 14, 1945. The next mission was finding and rescuing American POWs.

The war officially ended on September 2,1945, with a ceremony on the deck of the USS Missouri in Tokyo Bay. Curtis LeMay landed in Yokohama with an entourage and drove along streets in burned-out residential areas memorable for charred drill presses standing alone in the ashes, evidence of the cottage industry that had supported the war effort.[12] Thirty-eight years old at the time, he attended the surrender ceremony with generals who directed the war in the Pacific. The ceremony ended with an in-formation flyover of 462 B-29 bombers, which was undoubtedly an impressive display of military power.[13]

The war had changed America. Gone was isolationism; the US had the largest military in the world and the atom bomb, and the Air Force had been transformed from a subsidiary of the Army to the most powerful branch of the armed forces.

But there were headwinds. The country was in a demilitarizing frame of mind while the Soviet Union was going in the opposite direction, their technological development enhanced by the "acquisition" of scientists and engineers from Germany experienced in rocket and jet plane technology. LeMay was placed in charge of Air Force Research and Development in Washington, DC based on his ability to understand, communicate, and solve complex problems. His involvement led to the creation of a private company, Research and Development Corporation "Rand," located in California in close proximity to the companies that had produced so many military aircraft for the war effort.

His input in policy matters was noteworthy; in response to the dilemma of how the US would defend against a nuclear attack, he offered the first vision of Mutually Assured Destruction (MAD)[14]—the policy the US and Soviet Union followed through the Cold War—that the power to destroy an enemy needed to be so strong and impossible to stop that war was unthinkable. Which, it turns out, was the raison d'être for the 2,000 aircraft, nuclear-armed B-47 Fleet.

LeMay was the initial leader behind the Berlin Airlift, a fifteen-month (June 1948–September 1949) "exercise" to provide Berlin with supplies when the Soviets cut off road access to the jointly occupied city in East Germany.

Following that, in 1948 he was appointed Commander-in-Chief of the Strategic Air Command, the component of the Air Force responsible for nuclear weapons delivery. At that point in time SAC was in critical condition; everything—from lack of personnel training and morale, to equipment readiness and capability, to planning for an imminent attack—was in disarray and broken. During a simulated readiness test conducted in 1947, 101 of 180 planes could not get off the ground.[15]

LeMay, as frequently was the case, had the solution: clearly demonstrate the level of dysfunction, then use the results to isolate elements of the problem for improvement. So, he directed all bomber squadrons across the country to participate in a bombing exercise on Wright Field, Dayton, Ohio, with *inert, non-explosive, practice bombs*. The result: of all bombers actually able to fly to Dayton (some did not get off the ground) not one dropped bombs on target. His response: "'I've been telling you—you were in bad shape. We are in bad shape. Now let's get busy and get this fixed.'"[16]

"Training had to be radically changed to ensure that SAC crews could hit their assigned targets with the degree of accuracy required. Radar Bomb Scoring (RBS), first at fixed and then mobile sites, was a key element of the new emphasis on realistic training. Ground radar was used to track practice-bomb trajectories and location of impact. In 1947 there were only 880 scored bomb runs, but in 1949 the number rose to 28,049.

"By 1959, there were twenty-six RBS sites, twenty-one located in the United States and five outside the country. Those outside the United States were located at Montreal, London, San Juan, Guam, and Marrakech. The RBS sites were under the control of the Combat Evaluation Group (CEG) that was assigned to the 2nd Air Force at Barksdale AFB, Bossier Parish, Louisianna."[17]

Generally, the sites were in *remote areas* to reduce interference with civilian traffic and minimize noise complaints. Bomber crews were under pressure to hit the target. Consistency could earn spot promotions for the aircraft commander and navigator. A record of misses could lead, in the most extreme cases, to dismissal from the Air Force.[18]

LeMay realized that future conflicts would be entirely different from World War II, principally because more rapid means of weapon delivery—nuclear, by jet bomber and missiles—had erased the protection afforded by oceans of separation from potential enemies. His observation that "'SAC's first mission could very well be its last'"[19] required a state of readiness coinciding with the presumption that there would be only one chance to strike. This mind set, "'we are at war now,'"[20] presented in muted form by James Stewart in 1955 Paramount Picture's *Strategic Air Command* stirred fears in the American public and made LeMay a target for derision by those who favored an effort to find common ground with the Soviets. On the other side, those who accepted the notion of the Soviet's goal of world domination believed that LeMay was doing exactly the right thing.

The accident rate when LeMay became Commander-in-Chief of SAC in 1948 was 65 per 100,000 hours. In 1956, LeMay's last full year with SAC, it had dropped to 9 per 100,000 hours.[21] It would increase significantly as low-altitude bombing became the preferred approach. He institutionalized pre-flight inspections; set up classes for navigation, radar, and bombing; and required drills such as practice bombing runs. He also involved himself in promoting the succession of bomber aircraft, from the B-29 to the B-36, B-47, and finally the B-52, believing that there was no such thing as the ultimate weapon system.

By 1953, SAC had achieved the capability to deliver a massive preemptory strike. The fleet included 329 B-47s, 185 B-36s 500 air tankers (KC-97s) and 200 fighter planes. A global network of ten overseas bases had been developed, all within striking distance of the Soviet Union. There were twenty-nine bases in the US. Aircrews rotated on Alert Status with aircraft outside their accommodations ready to fly with nuclear arms at a moment's notice.[22]

In 1957, LeMay was promoted to Air Force Vice Chief of Staff. And that is about the time the real difficulties with the B-47 role as the primary nuclear weapons delivery aircraft began. Evolution of tactics was required.

LeMay was appointed Air Force Chief of Staff in 1961 by President Kennedy and after Kennedy's assassination served under President Lyndon Johnson until his retirement in 1965.

Following his retirement, he was American Independent Party Candidate George Wallace's running mate in the 1968 Presidential election. Wallace had been "'a sergeant in the Army Air Force, serving under General LeMay in the Pacific, and had flown combat missions on B-29s over Japan until he fell ill with spinal meningitis.'"[23] As governor of Alabama, he had gained nationwide recognition for his symbolic "schoolhouse-door" stand to block two African American women from registering for classes at the University of Alabama. At a time of racial tensions and riots, the assassination of Martin Luther King, and angst over the growing war in Vietnam, he became an advocate for "law and order," which attracted white voters who responded to his message from feelings of fear and racism.

Lt. Gen. Curtis LeMay and George Wallace—1968 Presidential Campaign. Photo by Bernard Gotfryd, Library of Congress/Prints and Photographs Division. Commons.

Invitations to join the campaign as the vice-presidential nominee were turned down by Texas Governor John Connolly and former governor "Happy" Chandler of Kentucky, among others. Initially reluctant to get involved, LeMay accepted the nomination in October 1968, a month before the election. While he held conservative views, there is no evidence that he was a racist—quite the opposite—but he feared he would be labeled as such by association with Wallace. LeMay's motivation was to prevent the Democratic party candidate, Hubert Humphrey, from winning because he viewed the Democratic party as soft on communism and likely to adversely affect the United States' strong strategic position.[24]

At the time LeMay joined the campaign, Wallace's support was surging and there was speculation that he might succeed in his objective: to prevent both Nixon and Humphrey from attaining a majority of electoral college votes, thus forcing the outcome to be decided in the House of Representatives, where Wallace could gain concessions from the candidate he supported.

LeMay's involvement turned out to be a disaster for Wallace's campaign. Not a politician by nature, at the initial press conference he talked about expanding the use of nuclear weapons and contradicted Wallace more than once when the latter interjected with comments that were intended to soften LeMay's remarks. The press conference was widely viewed as a debacle, and that, combined with the growth in popularity of Nixon and Humphrey, marked the end of the surge in support for Wallace.[25]

The Republican party ticket of Richard Nixon/Spiro Agnew defeated the Democratic Party ticket of Hubert Humphrey/Edmond Muskie. The popular vote was: Nixon 43.3 percent, Humphrey 42.7 percent, and Wallace 14 percent. Electoral votes for Nixon: 301, Humphrey: 191, Wallace: 46.[26] Wallace's strategy failed, but LeMay got what he wanted.

Curtis LeMay died on October 1, 1990, of complications from a heart attack in the 22nd Strategic Hospital on the grounds of March AFB, Riverside, California.[27] He is buried in the United States Air Force Academy Cemetery at Colorado Springs, Colorado. He served his country with fierce determination. May he rest in peace.

NOTES, CHAPTER 3:

[1] Eric Schmitt, "Iraq-Bound Troops Confront Rumsfeld Over Lack of Armor," *New York Times*, December 8, 2004.

[2] C. Mike Habermehl and Robert S. Hopkins III, *Boeing B-47 Stratojet: Strategic Air Command's Transitional Bomber* (Manchester, UK: Crecy Publishing, 2018), 9.

[3] Warren Kozak, *LeMay: The Life and Wars of General Curtis LeMay* (Washington, DC: Regnery Publishing, 2009).

[4] Ibid., xi.

[5] Ibid., 218.

[6] *The Fog of War: Eleven Lessons from the Life of Robert S. McNamara*, (documentary film) written and directed by Errol Morris, distributed by Sony Pictures Classics, released May 21 and December 19, 2003, Errol Morris: Film.

[7] Kozak, *LeMay*, 111.

[8] Ibid., 350.

[9] "Bomber on the Stump," *Time Magazine*, October 18, 1968.

[10] Warren Kozak, *LeMay*, 217.

[11] Ibid., 231.

[12] Ibid., 257.

[13] Ibid., 259.

[14] Ibid., 271.

[15] Ibid., 281.

[16] Ibid., 286.

[17] Sigmond Alexander, "Radar Bomb Scoring: RBS Operations," *The Stratojet Newsletter*, July 2005, 7.

[18] Ibid.

[19] Kozak, *LeMay*, 288.

[20] Ibid.

[21] Ibid., 291.

[22] Ibid., 308.

[23] Ibid., 368.

[24] Ibid., 371–374.

[25] Ibid., 375.

[26] Ibid., 381.

[27] Curtis Lemay, Curtis LeMay - Wikipedia.

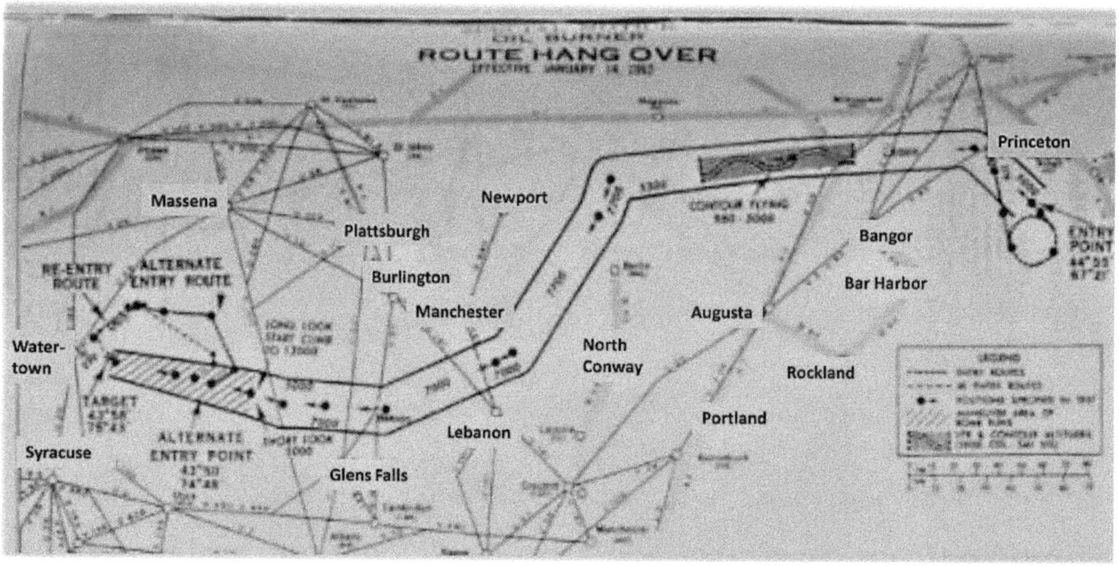

CHAPTER 4

THE EVOLUTION OF TACTICS: LOW-LEVEL BOMBING AND OIL BURNER TRAINING ROUTES

The failure of the LABS system of low-level bomb delivery and the need for an alternative drove a change in tactics and training, part of LeMay's legacy. As Air Force vice chief of staff, he undoubtedly exerted his considerable (!) influence to develop tactics that would address the growth of Soviet defensive capability.

Advances in Soviet air defense capabilities that included higher speed, all-weather fighters and surface-to-air missiles led to a re-evaluation of tactics by the Strategic Air Command, the primary target approach shifting from high to low altitude. Consistent with this, Oil Burner training routes became low-altitude, twelve converted by the end of 1959, and eventually all undergoing that change.

High-altitude training continued on a lower priority; by agreement with the Army Air Defense command, Nike surface-to-air missile sites were used by SAC aircrews for high altitude Radar Bomb Scoring practice.

Top: Oil Burner Hangover Route, Effective: January 14, 1962. Image: FAA Airman's Guide.[1] *Enhancements by Author.*

To make the low-level training more realistic, in 1961 mobile Radar Bomb Scoring was introduced, in which the "site" was mounted on a railway car that could be moved to unfamiliar locations, simulating bomb delivery challenges that would exist over enemy territory in wartime. Aiming points as references for releasing bombs were selected by the bombardier/navigator using maps; the approach under wartime conditions and success of the training mission was directly related to judgement in selection of the release point.[2]

While it had become clear that the B-47 aircraft, even in reinforced condition, could not continually endure the structural fatigue associated with the Low Altitude Bombing System (LABS), the need to approach the target at high speeds and low altitude remained. One element of the solution was Electronic Counter Measures (ECM), activated either by specially equipped aircraft accompanying the bombers or by systems carried in the bombers themselves. These systems were implemented by Strategic Air Command, the underlying principle of which was to confuse ground radar and associated weapons systems by creating a false target or a large zone of reflection that obscured multiple targets.

LOW-LEVEL BOMBING

At the same time, low-altitude bombing remained a primary tactic. The difference in procedure principally involved the way the bomb was delivered. Two variations in the high-speed, low-altitude tactics evolved.[3]

SHORT LOOK

A low-level approach, typically at an altitude of 500-1,000 feet over a 150- to 200-mile course, with electronic counter measures engaged close to the target. Airspeed on the approach increased from 320 mph to 450 mph with a maximum speed of 460 mph during the last five minutes. A short distance from the target the aircraft accelerated into a climb to 5,000 feet and at a calculated time released a nuclear bomb attached to a drogue chute. The purpose of the drogue chute was to slow the descent of the bomb to provide time for the aircraft to distance itself from the effects—radiation and blast wave—of the explosion.

To begin training for such missions the Aircraft commander (generally the pilot) was required to have 150 hours of B-47 experience, including 50 hours as AC. Certification required four sorties, the last at 500–1,000 feet elevation above mountainous terrain.

Dedicated "Oil Burner" routes, possibly so-named because jet engines of that era emitted highly visible smoke trails (particularly on takeoff when using water/alcohol injection to increase thrust) but perhaps also in recognition of the quantity of fuel consumed (1.5 billion gallons in 1957)[4] were approved by the FAA and time-restricted to avoid interference with peak commercial and general aviation use. Incidentally, 1.5 billion gallons of fuel would support fifty eight-hour flights/year of every B-47 in the 2,000-aircraft fleet. In 1959 training was expanded "to meet all operational circumstances including *night and instrument flight rules conditions (IFR).*"[5] Instrument-flight rules govern operation of aircraft when conditions are such that flying by visual reference is not safe, or perhaps not even possible. It was accomplished by use of flight-deck instrumentation and navigation-system radio-frequency signals from fixed ground sites.

LONG LOOK

The approach for this tactic was similar in altitude and speed; but instead of leveling out at 5,000 feet and releasing the weapon attached to a drogue chute, the acceleration and climb continued to 18,000 feet, where the weapon was released in free fall to the target. The additional altitude served the same purpose as the chute-associated time delay; it provided a means of escaping blast effects.[6]

*

In addition, SAC established two more bombing tactics for the B-47:

HIGH OR LOW ALTITUDE SYNCHRONOUS RADAR BOMBING

This is a bombing run where the aircraft and crew use the bomber's navigation, bombing system and radar to attack a target by finding and tracking the target's radar return or a radar return from an offset aiming point, from the initial point of the bomb run up to the weapon release point.[7]

LAST RESORT

Recognizing that under war-time conditions—which could result in no opportunity to abort a mission due to equipment failure, damage due to enemy action, or radar jamming by enemy countermeasures—last resort bombing was established in which the pilot or aircraft commander used a bombsight and a computed point of release. (In other words, releasing a bomb based on a visual reference.)

OIL BURNER TRAINING ROUTES

As time went on, the Strategic Air Command's focus shifted to the extent that high-altitude bombing was no longer in the war plan, and while it was thought necessary to remain proficient at high-altitude execution,[8] the Oil Burner routes were maintained primarily for low-altitude training.

In US airspace the number of Oil Burner routes increased to at least seventeen, more or less evenly distributed across the country in states like California (OB-16), Nevada (OB-10), Texas (OB-30), Florida (OB-77), and spanning states such as Oregon-Nevada (OB-1) and Montana-North Dakota (OB-24). Most, if not all, had colorful names, for example: Gun Load, Happy Hour, Rough Game, Steel Man, Bear Claws, Arrow Point, Derby Horse, Clear View, Ivory Tower, and Golf Tee. On the East Coast there was a "regional" route (OB-27) that began in Maine and went easterly through the northern parts of

New Hampshire, Vermont, and New York, terminating near Watertown, New York, at Fort Drum. The latter was the route frequently used by the SAC B-47 Squadron stationed at Plattsburgh Air Force Base, Plattsburgh, New York.

In the 1970s the "Oil Burner" designation was changed to "Olive Branch," partly in deference to the oil crisis but also in recognition of their deliberately heavy-handed—and successful—contribution to keeping the world peace.

OB-27 (a.k.a. the "Hangover") Oil Burner route[9] was possibly named because the need to reduce impact on civil use meant that training flights took place in early morning hours, thus leaving the crew with the feeling of a hangover the next day. The main entry point was in the vicinity of Bar Harbor, Maine, at 5,000 feet altitude, then traveling northwest; soon after turning west to the New Hampshire border and climbing to 5,300 feet; turning southwest and climbing to 7,300 feet, then descending to 7,000 feet at the New York State border; descending to 5,000 feet and flying west to the target in the Watertown-Fort Drum area. There, a simulated bombing attack with inert practice bombs was carried out—generally a "short look" at 490 mph airspeed.[10]

ECM jamming was active during the run. Following the run and a climb back to altitude, a right turn toward Massena was executed to get back on the "racetrack" (re-entry route) for the next run. There were usually multiple bombing runs followed by a wait to get scores, then a return to the Plattsburgh base via a climb-out route or possibly following high-altitude practice at the Buffalo, New York, Nike site.[11]

Multiple Nike surface-to-air missile sites defended the Buffalo area from possible attacks by Soviet bombers due to the connection between the Manhattan project—the US research project that produced the first atomic bomb—and industries located there, part of the nation's infrastructure necessary to produce nuclear weapons.[12] In the 1956–57 timeframe, Soviet aviation squadrons began receiving turboprop "Bear" bombers with a maximum speed of 510 mph (significantly less than the B-47) but a 9,000-mile operation range, far exceeding that of the B-47. Fortunately, the US military had initiated research and development on surface-to-air missiles in 1945, which was successfully completed in 1952 with a system test and demonstration. The first Nike missile battery became operational in December of 1953 at Fort Meade, Maryland. Missile sites in the Buffalo area were activated in 1955 and 1956. By 1957, 244 Nike batteries were in operation in the United States.[13]

There were eight Nike missile sites in the Buffalo area at: Model City, Cambria, Grand Island, Lockport, Millersport, Lancaster, Orchard Park, and Hamburg. The USAF SAGE (Semi-Automatic Ground Environment) radar station at the Lockport Air Force station was equipped with long-range radars and was connected to a computerized greater-air-surveillance network in the US Northeast. Early warning of hostile and friendly aircraft was normally passed to the Nike Sites.[14] Practice Alert Status drills and inspections were frequent, as were multiday "war games" that exercised the full chain of command and included the USAF and the Navy. It is therefore reasonable to conclude that a Buffalo

Nike Site selected for high-altitude bombing practice was aware of the mission and may, in some way, have used it as a training exercise.[15]

There was also a USAF BOMARC [48 missile], anti-aircraft site on what was the Niagara Falls Air Force base.[16]

In the early morning hours of January 16, 1962, the B-47 with Pilot Rodney Bloomgren, Copilot Melvin Spencer, Navigator Albert Kandetski and Observer Kenneth Jensen on board completed the navigation route, took two high-altitude passes at the Watertown site and then made a fateful decision to reenter the bomb run for a "short look," rather than return directly to Plattsburgh Air Force base or visit the Buffalo area Nike installations.

NOTES, CHAPTER 4:

[1] Federal Aviation Agency, *Airman's Guide* 17, no. 1, (March 13, 1962): 17-Special.

[2] Sigmund Alexander, "Radar Bomb Scoring: RBS Operations," *The Stratojet Newsletter*, July 2005, 7.

[3] C. Mike Habermehl and Robert S. Hopkins III, *Boeing B-47 Stratojet: Strategic Air Command's Transitional Bomber* (Manchester, UK: Crecy Publishing, 2018),107. [4]Warren Kozak, *LeMay: The Life and Wars of General Curtis LeMay* (Washington, DC: Regnery Publishing, 2009), 327.

[5] Habermehl and Hopkins, *Boeing B-47—SAC's Traditional Bomber*, 107.

[6] Ibid.

[7] Frank Baehre, in communication with the author, December 4, 2023.

[8] Sigmund Alexander, "Memories of a Navigator," http///b-47.com/wp-content/uploads/2012/03/Memories.pdf.

[9] Ibid.

[10] Ibid.

[11] Ibid.

[12] Paul Robitaille, "Part 1-The Gun Era," in *History of the Niagara-Buffalo Army Air Defense 1952–1970*, The Nike Historical Society, 2, www. nikemissile.org/NFBU52-70.pdf. 2.

[13] Ibid., Part 2-The "Nike Missile" Era, 1.

[14] Ibid.,12.

[15] Paul Robitaille, in communication with the author, July 15, 2021.

[16] Frank Baehre, in communication with the author, December 4, 2023

CHAPTER 5

PLATTSBURGH AIR FORCE BASE

Plattsburgh, New York, is located in the extreme northeast corner of New York State, twenty miles from the Canadian Border, on the eastern shore of Lake Champlain, across the lake from Burlington, Vermont.

Plattsburgh Air Force Base was established on the 140-year-old Plattsburgh Military Reservation by the Strategic Air Command in July 1955, a result of persistent lobbying by Mr. Clyde Lewis, a much-decorated WWII US Army Air Corps B-17 squadron commander and community leader. At the same time, the 528th, 529th and 530th bombardment squadrons were activated and assigned to the 380th Bombardment Wing, which included the 380th Air Refueling Squadron.[1]

The main runway direction is designated 17/35, meaning compass bearings 170/350; true north is 360, south is 180, so north/south for all practical purposes. With a length of 11,758 feet (2.2 miles) it was long enough to accommodate a B-47 takeoff. Elevation above mean sea level is 234 feet.[2]

The first B-47E arrived there on March 21, 1956, followed by the KC-97 tankers of the Air Refueling Squadron. Sixteen B-47s were initially assigned to the Wing. This grew to a peak of seventy B-47s and forty KC-97s by July 1959. The 380th Wing was declared combat-ready in October 1956.[2]

Top: Plattsburgh Air Force Base in Plattsburgh, New York—May 4, 1994. Image: USGS, Wikipedia.

During the Cuban Missile Crisis of October 1962, the 380th Wing, along with bombers at all SAC bases, were prepared for war. "Nuclear weapons were often seen on the flight line, but this was different. They were everywhere as all the planes were being uploaded."[3,4]

As the deployment of ICBMs and B-52 bombers increased, the role of the B-47 gradually diminished, and the era of the B-47 in the "North Country" ended. On December 14, 1965, the last three departed. coinciding closely with the retirement of all SAC B-47 bombers. The final flight of a B-47, a B-47E, occurred on June 17,1986, from the Naval Air Weapons Station at China Lake, California, to Castle Air Force Base in California's San Joaquin Valley, with experienced USAF B-47 pilots Major General John D. Moore and Lieutenant Colonel Dale E. Wolfe at the controls. Because the B-47E had not been through a complete overhaul prior to the flight, the landing gear remained extended throughout, reflecting an abundance of caution. In an echo from the past, during the 43-minute trip the aircraft had several systems fail, including airspeed sensors, intercom, and partial aileron control. Following the flight, the aircraft was placed on permanent display, at the Castle Air Museum.[5]

The Air Force base closed in 1995, one in a series of base closures reflecting the growth of missile weapon systems and a desire by the federal government for increased efficiency and related cost-cutting in military activity via the Base Realignment and Closure Commission (BRAC). It was a heartbreaking affair for the citizens of that region, playing out over a four-year period starting with the commission decisions in 1991 when Plattsburgh was spared, then culminating with a last-minute decision to close in 1993. People lined the streets along the route taken by commission members when they came for hearings, and the meeting room was packed. As there had been talk with the Air Force about base expansion just prior to the closure decision, the community leadership felt blindsided.[6]

While the region has recovered economically, there remains a sense of loss of diversity associated with the presence of military personnel and their families.[7]

Crowds line BRAC commission's route to PAFB. © Nancie Battaglia.

BRAC Commission Hearing—PAFB. © Nancie Battaglia.

Plattsburgh Air Force Base Museum. © Nancie Battaglia 2021.

The former base is now a civilian airport and mixed-use industrial site with repurposed base buildings, including three museums on the Old Base Museum campus: Clinton County Historical Museum, Plattsburgh Air Force Base Museum, and the War of 1812 Museum. With the Air Force unlikely to ever return, community members have taken action to keep the legacy alive.

The original Plattsburgh Air Force Base Museum closed together with the base, and all the artifacts and exhibits were taken to the National Air Force Museum in Dayton, Ohio. In 2013, in a move to preserve the Air Force Base legacy, a group of former Air Force military and civilian personnel, community members, and SUNY Plattsburgh students began the effort to reopen the museum at the original site, collecting artifacts from other retired Air Force personnel and making exhibits documenting base history from a large collection of slides. Among the artifacts and exhibits are: an inert, non-explosive 750-pound training shape bomb; a FB-111 cockpit procedure training module; a video of the last KC-135 refueling mission; an operating (noisy) klaxon that signaled the beginning of an Alert Status bombing exercise; an operating Atlas missile launch control console; a collection of trophies won by the Plattsburgh Air Force team at annual SAC competitions, including the Fairchild trophy for outstanding bomb unit; and the control yoke and a landing gear wheel from the B-47 that crashed at Wright Peak.[8] The museum, now open to the public at 31 Washington Drive, is within easy walking distance of the Clyde Lewis Airpark, where the B-47 bomber *Pride of the Adirondacks*, an award winner at the 1965 Fairchild competition, and an FB-111A are on display.

During their stay at Plattsburgh, the 380th B-47 squadrons distinguished themselves at competitions held at the Paris Air Show, and at SAC's Fairchild Air Force Base, Washington. They also participated in grueling Alert Status and Reflex exercises to maintain the ability to act on short notice if war was imminent. Quite naturally, the name of the roadway to the barracks where the crews on Alert Status were quartered was LeMay Drive.

Unfortunately, like all other Air Force bases, Plattsburgh suffered losses of crewmen and aircraft. The first accident occurred on July 18, 1957 when a KC-97 tanker with a crew of eight exploded and crashed

Pride of the Adirondacks B-47E, Clyde Lewis Airpark, Plattsburgh, NY. ©Nancie Battaglia 2021.

FB-111A, Clyde Lewis Airpark, Plattsburgh, NY. ©Nancie Battaglia 2021.

into Lake Champlain after two of four engines failed three minutes from takeoff. There were five fatalities.[9] Other accidents involving Plattsburgh AFB B-47s that resulted in fatalities included:

> 9/17/1957 – Loss of control when returning from a mission resulted in the "airplane rolling repeatedly up to a 60-degree bank,"[10] which could not be overcome by all efforts on the part of the aircraft commander (AC) and copilot. "Mayday was declared. Eventually the AC ordered the crew to eject. The aircraft was abandoned in the Gulf of St. Lawrence between Nova Scotia and Newfoundland. Co-pilot ejected and was rescued from a raft. Two other crewmen were never found."[11]

> 1/5/1959 – "Dragged wing during cross wind takeoff."[12] Aircraft destroyed in a crash when the left wing dropped; the pilot corrected, and the aircraft rolled to the right. The aircraft

repeated a roll to the left, the left wing hit the ground and the aircraft exploded. The copilot was killed. Three others on board were injured.[13]

9/14/1960 – Mid-air collision. A needless accident occurred when a copilot requested that a second B-47 flying in formation maneuver close so a home movie could be filmed. A wingtip and outboard engine of the second airplane hit the first, causing it to become "uncontrollable and crash into the Atlantic Ocean."[14] "Part of a three-ship cell heading for Brize Norton…300 miles west of Shannon, Ireland [when the accident occurred]. The three-man crew were never found and were presumed to have been killed. Unknown whether any of them ejected."[15] The second plane landed safely at Shannon, Ireland.

1/16/1962 – "A Boeing B-47 Stratojet on low-altitude bombing run training mission, is reported overdue at 0700 hrs. Last radio call was at ~0200 hrs. After four-day search, wreckage is spotted in the Adirondack High Peaks. Bomber clipped the top of Wright Peak (16th tallest mountain in the Adirondacks, at 4580 feet) after veering 30 miles off course in inclement weather, high winds."[16]

The description of the accident at Wright Peak, commonly referred to as a Controlled Flight into Terrain (CFIT) is perplexing. Use of the phrase *"after veering 30 miles off course"* immediately raises questions. More on that later.

While CFIT occurrences involving crashes into mountains or mountainous terrain were a relatively small contribution to the total number of B-47 accidents, there are some common causal factors that stand out. Failures in navigation, not necessarily human, and altimeter errors are among the reasons cited, though for other crashes the cause(s) are unknown. During the years the B-47 was operational there were six, three of which occurred in 1962.

The first accident happened on April 7, 1957, when "[B-47 serial #] 51-2425 of the 96th BW [Altus AFB, OK] crashed into Kaala Mountain on approach to Hickam AFB, Hawaii….4 crewmen killed."[17] Returning from Guam, the aircraft encountered engine problems and diverted course to Hickam. The crew lacked the chart for an instrument approach, so the control tower gave instructions verbally. The AC (pilot) repeated them but mistakenly said a right turn for alignment to the inbound flight path rather than left. This was challenged by the control tower but not acknowledged by the AC. Problems had been reported earlier by the crew about the radio, which may have been the reason for presumably not receiving the challenge. The airplane turned right and crashed into Ka'ala mountain at 4:00 a.m., fifty feet below the summit.[18] Certain aspects of this accident, loss of radio contact and lack of instructions for navigation, are similar to that of the Wright Peak crash.

Interestingly, while descriptions of other accidents involving collisions with mountains and views of wreckage accessed from hiking trails are common in media sources, there is a dearth of such information pertaining to the B-47 crash site on Ka'ala mountain, though the wreckage of B-24 *Evelyn* is visited by hikers and well-known. Perhaps the B-47 wreckage was removed.

The second collision with a mountain came late the same year in California. "Palomar Mountain, Calif. (AP)—A fiery bomber crash in fog about a quarter-mile from the 200-inch world's biggest telescope has left three Air Force officers dead. The six-engine B-47 Stratojet was returning to March Air Force Base, 50 miles to the north, from a training flight. Flames shot 100 feet high and live ammunition went off, an observatory official said. Flying debris nicked the dome of a smaller telescope, the 48-inch Schmidt."[19, 20] "The accident investigation revealed that the aircraft was 8 miles off course and 5,000 feet below minimums for the approach the aircraft was flying."[21] No explanation for these errors is readily available. As of 2008, some of the wreckage still existed on private lands.

On June 11, 1958, another crash occurred involving a B-47 on instrument approach, this time to Plattsburgh Air Force Base. "The aircraft [#1931] was en-route to Loring, Me. prior to going Reflex. [It] diverted to Plattsburgh because of weather in the Loring area...one of several attempting to make GCA [Ground Control Approach] landings at Plattsburgh. The Plattsburgh GCA had trouble making positive contact with #1931 and directed the aircraft to climb to 5,000 feet on a heading of 170 degrees. The pilot acknowledged the transmission and that was the last transmission that was heard from him. The aircraft crashed near Enosburg, Vt [on Cold Hollow Mountain] killing all 4 aboard. The aircraft was found to be in a near vertical bank to the left, nose down. The investigation concluded the disorientation resulting from loss of control was the primary cause."[22] The site is accessible by hiking.

After a four-year gap in collisions with mountains, on January 16, 1962, a B-47 assigned to Plattsburgh AFB crashed on Wright Peak. Then, on July 23, 1962:

> "An Air Force B-47 bomber left Dyess Air Force Base near Abilene, Texas, around 6:30 that night for a routine training mission through Montana. Four men were on board. Radio transcripts and maps of the flight path show they flew around Dillon and crossed the Paradise Valley. They were supposed to turn to the northeast, but instead their plane slammed into the southwestern slope of Emigrant Peak, about 8,500 feet up, creating a fireball. Officially, the cause of the crash is undetermined. Air Force documents obtained by the Bozeman Chronicle through a public records request say the most probable cause is an error by some member of the crew, but they can't say for sure. More than 20 pages in the investigation are blacked out, and it's likely no one will ever know exactly what caused the wreck. Debris scattered everywhere. The explosion started a wildfire, which the Livingston Enterprise reported grew to about 40 acres.
>
> All four of the men died in the crash, their lives cut short more than a thousand miles from their base. There was Capt. Bill Faulconer, a one-time Price is Right contestant from Kansas who thought he'd start farming once he left the Air Force. There was Lt. Fred Hixenbaugh, a West Virginian who used to prank his sisters and loved baseball. There was Lt. David Sutton, from Oklahoma, who was exactly one month into his second year as a full pilot. And there

was Lt. Lloyd Sawyers, a Texan who would save the box dinners he got on missions for his two young daughters.

Damage from the fire was fairly minimal, but the wreckage spread out across a good chunk of the mountain, about 2,500 feet below the top. Clean-up crews didn't pick up everything they found, so remnants of the plane are still there, now as much a part of the landscape as the trees themselves."[23]

"For some unknown reason the crew descended below the minimum published altitude of 15,000 feet"[24]

"President Donald Trump signed the B-47 Designation Act passed by Congress on Tuesday [October 18, 2020] naming the area east of Paradise Valley the 'B-47 Ridge.'"[25]

Finally, on August 23, 1962 a B-47 from Davis-Monthan AFB, Arizona, at the entry point of an Oil Burner route and cleared for a "short look" simulated bomb release, crashed in a slight descent 200 vertical feet from the summit of a mountain near Smith's Ferry Indiana. All crewmen perished. Published minimum altitude for the route segment was 2,700 feet *above* the point of impact. No reason is readily available for the accident.[26]

As mentioned previously and evident in the foregoing descriptions, there is some commonality in the causes of B-47 collisions with mountainous terrain. What *appear* to be clear failures in navigation—in altitude and/or location—are contained in the descriptions of:

- Emigrant Mountain, (6,500 feet altitude error);
- Mt. Palomar (errors of 5,000 feet altitude, eight miles off course);
- Wright Peak (thirty miles off course); and
- Smith's Ferry (2,700 feet altitude error).

It is difficult to explain how errors of that magnitude can occur, which is supported by the fact that in the cases of Emigrant Mountain, Smith's Ferry, and Mt. Palomar *no official explanation for the crash exists.* One wonders if the crew simply lost control of the aircraft for a variety of reasons including mechanical failures, and the mountain just happened to be the place where it impacted with terrain. The absence of official explanations is in contrast with:

- The cause of the crash on Ka'ala Mountain stands out as a simple matter of radio communication failure.
- Cold Hollow Mountain crash was officially attributed to crew disorientation.
- *The official explanation for the Wright Peak tragedy is much more complicated.*

NOTES, CHAPTER 5:

[1] SAC Bases-Plattsburgh AFB: 380th Bomb Wing—B-47, B-52, FB111A, strategic-air-command.com.

[2] Plattsburgh Air Force Base: https://military-history.fandom.com/wiki/Plattsburgh__Air-Force__Base.

[3] SAC Bases.

[4] People Near Here – Plattsburgh Airforce Base Reunion: https://mountainlake.org/people-near-here-plattsburgh-airforce-base-reunion/.

[5] This Day in Aviation, https://thisdayinaviation.com/17-june-1986

[6] Joe LoTemplio, "Decision to Close PAFB Blindsided Community," *Plattsburgh Press-Republican*, September 26, 2015.

[7] Pat Bradley, "A Look Back at Plattsburgh Air Force Base Closure Twenty Years Ago," *WAMC Northeast Public Radio*, September 25, 2015.

[8] Franklin Baehre, Curator, Plattsburgh Air Force Base Museum, in communication with the author, 10/7/2021.

[9] "SAC Bases-Plattsburgh AFB: 380th Bomb Wing—B-47, B-52, FB111A," strategic-air-command.com.

[10] C. Mike Habermehl and Robert S. Hopkins III, *Boeing B-47 Stratojet: Strategic Air Command's Transitional Bomber* (Manchester, UK: Crecy Publishing, 2018), 289.

[11] B-47 Historical Website, B-47 Losses https://b-47.com/wp-content/uploads/2014/03/Boeing -b47-losses-and-ejections.pdf.

[12] Habermehl and Hopkins, *Boeing B-47—SAC's Transitional Bomber*, 278.

[13] B-47 Historical Website, B-47 Losses https://b-47.com/wp-content/uploads/2014/03/Boeing -b47-losses-and-ejections.pdf.

[14] Habermehl and Hopkins, *Boeing B-47—SAC's Transitional Bomber*, 288.

[15] B-47 Historical Website, B-47 Losses https://b-47.com/wp-content/uploads/2014/03/Boeing -b47-losses-and-ejections.pdf.

[16] List of accidents and incidents involving military aircraft (1960–1969) - Wikipedia, January 16, 1962.

[17] 1951 USAF Serial Numbers (joebaugher.com), 51-2425.

[18] Habermehl and Hopkins, *Boeing B-47—SAC's Transitional Bomber*, 286.

[19] "B47 CRASHES NEAR GIANT OBSERVATORY," *the Ada Evening News* (Oklahoma) December 19,1957, Palomar Mountain, CA Bomber Crash, Dec 1957 | GenDisasters ... Genealogy in Tragedy, Disasters, Fires, Floods.

[20] Robert Lerner, "Remembering Valley Center's air disasters," *Valley Roadrunner (hometown newspaper)*, September 5, 2019, Remembering Valley Center's air disasters - Valley Roadrunner https://www.valleycenter.com/articles/remembering-Valley-Center's-air-disasters.

[21] B-47 Historical Website, B-47 Losses https://b-47.com/wp-content/uploads/2014/03/Boeing -b47-losses-and-ejections.pdf.

[22] Ibid.

[23] Michael Wright, "Debris remains on Emigrant Peak from 1962 bomber crash," *Bozeman Daily Chronicle*, July 17, 2016, https://www.bozemandailychronicle.com/news/in-memory-of-a-plane-crash/article__b821f15f-ecee-5d19-baac-0f1ead5c9edc.html.

[24] Habermehl and Hopkins, *Boeing B-47—SAC's Transitional Bomber*, 292.

[25] "Montana ridge named in honor of airmen who died in 1962 B-47 crash," *Associated Press*, October 18, 2020.

[26] Habermehl and Hopkins, *Boeing B-47—SAC's Transitional Bomber*, 294.

CHAPTER 6

THE WRIGHT PEAK ACCIDENT

FIRST, A QUICK SUMMARY—

The condensed version of the story is based on a 1983 *Adirondack Life* article,[1] which references an "Investigation Board" and contains information from the "final report issued by the Air Force," the latter very likely to be the US Air Force Accident/Incident Report available by Freedom of Information Act (FOIA) request. In summary it states that a B-47 stationed at Plattsburgh Air Force Base vanished after participating in bomb delivery practice at Fort Drum, near Watertown, New York. There were four aboard, a crew of three and a maintenance observer. The last contact with the plane was at 2:00 a.m., when it radioed the Boston Federal Aviation Administration Center that it was taking an alternate flight path home. The radar unit at Fort Drum received word at 8:00 a.m. on January 16, 1962 that the plane was missing.

Numerous tips were provided to the New York State Police in Malone New York, following a request to the public for any information on an unusual sighting or noise during the previous night. Some accounts were realistic enough to be investigated by a search party, but none yielded useful information. By January 20 there were fifty aircraft involved in the search. On Sunday the 21st, a wing, three parachutes, and scattered debris across the summit of Wright Mountain were spotted. A rescue team

Top: Wright Peak (Elev. 4,580 ft.) and Algonquin (Elev. 5,144 ft.), Left to Right. © Nancie Battaglia 2021.

hiked toward the summit of Wright but was driven back by a combination of low visibility and severe ice and snow conditions. Likewise, dog sled teams were unsuccessful in reaching the area of the crash. On Monday, a search party was able to reach the top and found that the debris path extended down the southeast side of the mountain, but there were no large pieces of wreckage, such as portions of the fuselage, and no survivors. On Tuesday, a team of fifty men explored the crash site. Remains of the pilot and copilot were found.

The Investigation Board findings were that:

1. "The low-level route being used did not allow for use of radio navigation aids."
2. "Crew distraction with the weather and turbulence, along with probable failure of the altimeter, also contributed."

> "The board's feelings were that the lack of Radio Navigation Aids was the primary cause. The aircraft was off course and without radio assistance was not aware of it. And upon beginning descent into the low-level route, crashed."[2]

NOW THE DETAILS—

More details from the investigative USAF Accident/Incident Report[3] referenced above are of interest. The following is a summary of the report, obtained via FOIA procedure from the USAF, with liberties taken to change military terminology to more familiar terms (e.g., speed in "knots" to miles per hour, military time to standard time).

B-47E serial number 53-2119, call sign Pete 67, was assigned to the 380th Bombardment Wing, Plattsburgh Air Force Base. Crew members assigned to the 529th Bombardment Squadron were: Aircraft Commander First Lieutenant Rodney D. Bloomgren; Copilot, First Lieutenant Melvin Spencer; and Navigator, First Lieutenant Albert W. Kandetski. Airman First Class Kenneth R. Jensen, an airborne *electronics equipment repairman* of the 380th Armament and Electronics Maintenance was aboard as an observer.

According to the Flying Experience record, pilot/AC 1st Lt. Bloomgren had a total of 1,266 hours of experience, with 1,023 in a B-47, of which 204 were in "Weather Instrument," and had flown 28 hours in the last thirty days. Copilot 1st Lt. Spencer's experience was just slightly lower: 1,030 total; 657 B-47; 196 Weather Instrument; 23 in the last thirty days.[4] First Lt. Kandetski: 612 total as navigator and navigator/bombardier.[5] Altogether, not the most experienced crew flying B-47s but with a reasonable number of flight hours (some under weather-related instrument conditions) and flight experience in the region of the crash.

Aircraft Commander Bloomgren had been assigned to Plattsburgh Air Force Base in September[6] and had accumulated 64 hours of flying in the previous ninety days there.[7] One would expect that he had some knowledge of the mountainous terrain south-southwest of the Base—the High Peaks of the Adirondacks—as training would have included practice bombing runs on the Watertown RBS site via the Hangover Oil Burner route.

The briefing for the mission was conducted three days previously per established procedures, and no immediate issues were identified.

However, in two sections of the report, "Technical Orders Compliances Not Complied With"[8] and "Discrepancies Reported by the Pilot for Last 5 Flights Prior to Accident,"[9] there are indications of ongoing reliability problems with critical avionics systems, specifically the radar altimeter, radar scope, and VOR radio navigation system.

The VOR (short for Very high-frequency Omnidirectional Range) system was the primary means for navigation under low (or no) visibility conditions. The ground-based VOR system transmits a circular pattern of radial radio "beams" at one-degree increments as directional guidance for aircraft with the proper receiving equipment.

The avionics problems were corrected prior to the fateful flight by the simple means of component replacement and tightening of connections but are suggestive of the reason an electronics repairman was an observer onboard.

Known as a "maintenance hog," to quote one contributor to the B-47 Historical Website (B-47 Operations) on the subject of avionics reliability: "[The vacuum tube radio] being mounted in the B-47 tail and exposed to the chill of high altitude sure didn't help reliability one bit. But I guess almost all of the avionics in the B-47 was mounted outside of the pressurized compartment and suffered accordingly."[10]

One could second guess the decision to fly that night on the basis that severe turbulence would tend to make the reliability of electronics systems worse.

History of the Flight summary—[11]

Arrival of the flight crew at 2130 hrs. (9:30 p.m.) on January 15 was followed by preflight preparations, which identified an "inoperative high frequency (HF) radio." A HF radio enables communications that would not be possible by systems requiring an unobstructed line of sight between transmitting and receiving locations. The RT (receiver transmitter) of the radio was replaced, and proper operation was verified. *Later, the radio or a subsystem would apparently fail intermittently during critical moments of the flight.*

A weather briefing was completed at 10:15 p.m. It was not an ideal night for a flight, particularly near mountainous terrain. Due to the existence of fronts passing through the region, winds were predicted to be very strong at takeoff with moderate turbulence and overcast at 3,000 feet expected, and light rain showers. A jet stream near the intended flight path with winds 150 mph from the west-southwest was reported to be in the Albany area with the possibility of "Clear Air Turbulence." The Watertown alternate entry to the Oil Burner Hangover route was forecast to be 1,000–1,500 feet overcast (and in the crash area tops of clouds were estimated to be at 8,000 to 10,000 feet), two miles visibility (below the cloud layer) with snow showers and unstable conditions. Most importantly, *the rapidly changing conditions required that the crew contact Plattsburgh Metro Weather station to obtain sea level pressure on which the pressure altimeter calibration is based,* before re-entering the route.

Engines were started at 10:50 p.m., and a fuel-flow fluctuation was detected in number-two engine. All other measures of engine health were normal, so it was concluded that the flow indicator was malfunctioning—*another electrical glitch*.

The aircraft was cleared for takeoff and departed for a high-level practice-bomb-delivery training run at 11:33 p.m. The crew reported Visual Flight Rules (VFR) above cloud layer to Burlington Air Traffic Control (ATC) and was instructed to contact Boston Federal Aviation Agency Center for a flight conditions update. The scheduled training exercise had two distinct parts—a navigation portion and a training "long look" bombing run.

The flight proceeded as planned on a navigation training path to Berlin, NH; thence including Albany, New York; Allentown, Pennsylvania; Albany, New York; Plattsburgh, New York; Watertown, New York; and finally, the Oil Burner Hangover entry point in the vicinity of Indian Lake, New York, with an apparent scheduled time of arrival of 1:55 a.m. At that location the aircraft was to climb to 13,000 feet (above mean sea level) in accordance with *Airman's Guide* route definition.[12]

The Watertown Radar Bomb Scoring (RBS) site reported two (inert bomb) releases from Pete 67 at 1:43 and 1:46 a.m., the first twelve minutes ahead of schedule.

The aircraft crew then informed the RBS site of their intention to make a "short look" release at 2:18 a.m. and advised that they would contact the Boston FAA Center for clearance. One is led to believe that it was unusual to follow a higher-altitude "long look" bombing run with a "short look" based on a description contained in the Airman's Guide.[16] In any event, at 1:57 a.m. permission for immediate reentry to the Oil Burner route was requested and sea level pressure reference of 29.99 inches mercury was provided for altimeter setting; at that time the aircraft was "4 miles out from the Watertown VOR [air traffic navigation transmitter center]"; the Boston FAA Center directed Pete 67 to contact Watertown [Air Traffic Control]. No contact was made [with Watertown] but at approximately 2:05 a.m. Pete 67 contacted Plattsburgh Metro [ATC] for Watertown forecast pressure and radar calibration data, at 5,000 and 13,000 feet. No further contacts were made to any entity. The aircraft collided with Wright Peak thirty-five feet below the summit and disintegrated on impact with the vertical granite ledge. The crew perished on impact. An explosion and fire occurred. The estimated time of the impact was 2:10 a.m.

The summit elevation of Wright peak is 4,580 feet. The photo below shows the impact area approximately fifty yards northwest of the summit; the vertical ledge at the center of the encircled area is the point of impact, indicating that the aircraft was flying significantly below the intended altitude of 5,000 feet and confirming the estimate of 35 feet below the summit elevation. Also note the image of Mt. Marcy in the background, which the plane had no hope of clearing even if flying at 5,000 feet.

The Investigative Board identified in specific terms that "*the primary cause factor of this accident was that the crew allowed the aircraft to deviate sufficiently from the published alternate entry to the Oilburner Hangover low level navigation route that, upon descending to the published level off* [sic—of?] *altitude, the*

Wright Peak crash site (encircled). Mt. Marcy at upper center of photo. © Nancie Battaglia 2021.

aircraft was below the peaks of the surrounding terrain."[13] This is a somewhat different statement than contained in the Adirondack Life Article,[14] in essence placing some of the blame for the accident on the crew's navigation and/or operation of the aircraft. A thorough examination of the evidence suggests that the crew had a specific reason for deviation from the alternate entry.

Continuing, the Board listed contributing factors that included: a) lack of radio navigational aids to accurately monitor aircraft position during entrance to the Oil Burner Hangover route; b) insufficient time scheduled between high altitude (practice) bomb release and route entry causing distraction of the crew during the critical descent portion; c) weather that obscured mountain tops in clouds, including probable severe turbulence over the summits; and d) *a computed altimeter error of 440 feet that placed the aircraft well below its intended 5,000 feet altitude*.

Looking at the accident at a higher level of detail, there are several pieces to the puzzle of reasons for the crash:

1. Timeline of activity following bombing run.
2. Miscalibration of pressure altimeter.
3. Unfavorable weather conditions: turbulence, cloud layer/lack of visibility.
4. Flight path taken from Watertown to Wright Peak.

5. Intermittent radio communications during the flight.
6. Deviation from the alternate entry route.
7. Re-entry Point Altitude Specification.
8. Terrain Avoidance Radar (TAR).
9. Location of the turn toward southeast.

Summarizing information from various sources address the pieces of this puzzle:

1. Timeline of aircraft activity following the bombing run.[15]

- 1:46 a.m.—Final release of high-altitude practice bombs.
- 1:57 a.m.—Four miles out from the Watertown VOR (navigational transmitter station).
- 2:05 a.m.—Contact with Plattsburgh Metro Air Traffic Control for altimeter calibration data.
- 2:10 a.m.—Accident Report: *approximate* time of impact with Wright Peak.

The first three are based on information from reliable, on-ground sources. The fourth is an estimate, labeled *approximate* without definition of source. This lack of precision is noteworthy and leads to speculation. Was it the best estimate of the time when an air traffic control observer at Plattsburgh Metro noticed that an unidentified aircraft image on a radar scope vanished at a VOR radial/compass bearing corresponding to that of Wright Peak? *Or more probably, it was based on radar tracking information reportedly in the possession of the Air Force.*[16]

2. Miscalibration of pressure altimeter. Quoting from the Official USAF Accident Report:

> "Since it is the practice among crews, on short entry runs, to set in the forecast altimeter setting received from the forecaster at PFSV [Pilot to Forecaster SerVice], it is reasonable to assume that the aircraft had 29.98 as a Kohlsman [*sic*—Kollsman] setting. This would have resulted in an indicated altimeter error of approximately [minus] 440 feet."[17]

Author's Note: a "Kollsman" is a pressure altimeter, named after the inventor. The setting is the reference or base pressure that adjusts the gauge to accurately indicate altitude above sea level.

Actually, the Kollsman setting of 29.98 is only one factor, and a relatively small contribution to the altitude error. It corrects the altimeter setting for the sea level pressure deviation from that of the "Standard Atmosphere", which is 29.92. In this case resulting in a negative altitude error of 60 feet. The other factor is the "D" factor, which corrects for deviations from the Standard Atmosphere due to local weather conditions, not addressed in the above section of the report. The weather history extracted value for the

D factor at the location of the crash was negative 380 feet, so in combination the estimated altimeter error was -440 feet.

At the instant of impact, the altimeter was in all likelihood reading 5,000 feet—the altitude for entry to the low-level bombing run. The combined altitude error would place the aircraft at 4,560 feet, 20 feet below the summit elevation of Wright Peak and close to the estimated impact point elevation of 4,545 feet.

3. Weather conditions.

"Probable severe turbulence, moderate icing, in-cloud conditions along track taken immediately before the accident."[18] Wind speed at 5,000 feet altitude was estimated to be 50 knots (57 mph)—not, by itself, an issue.

The B-47 was known as a fair-weather bomber; it could be difficult to control under the best of conditions. The crew would have had their hands full simply in the effort to maintain control in severe turbulence and the fact that it was flying in at cloud layer eliminated visual navigation and use of a sextant to ascertain location.

The cloud layer near the impact point extended from 2,000 feet to 8,000–10,000 feet, making it impossible to see the mountain summit.

4. Flight path from Watertown to Wright Peak.

Available information on the track followed just prior to the impact on Wright Peak is consistent from two sources:

First, "officials [unnamed] at the [Wright Peak Accident] scene estimated that the bomber was flying in a direct path towards Marcy—[in other words southeast]—when it struck Wright a point 35 feet from the uppermost rock shelf hitting at about a 70-degree angle head-on."[19]

This supports the statement on the flight path immediately before the accident from the primary source: "The track flown was from approximately 20 miles northwest of the crash point to the crash point."[20]

The basis for the information on the track prior to the crash must have been radar tracking. Taking it at face value, the aircraft had been flying in the southeast direction for twenty miles. The reference to twenty miles northwest of the crash point suggests a turn from a segment of the flight path not in the southeast direction. Since the flight path origin was Watertown, a reasonable conclusion is that the plane flew in the east-northeast direction toward Plattsburgh, then made a turn southeast twenty miles from the crash site shortly after contact with Plattsburgh Metro.

Information on ground speed at time of impact tends to confirm the above. A response to an October 8, 1989 Associated Press article "Remnants of '62 Crash Litter Peak" in the Plattsburgh Press-Republican[21] by an individual identifying himself as a member of the Accident Investigation Board states that the aircraft was traveling at "approximately 377 knots (434 mph) ground speed" at the time of impact.[22]

Lacking any information on ground speed from the aircraft crew just prior to impact or a flight recorder—neither existing—the only reasonable basis for such an estimate would be knowledge of the flight path and the elapsed time to complete the segments: a) Watertown to the turn southeast, and b) the turn southeast to the impact with Wright Peak. Based on 434 mph ground speed from the location of the turn to impact, the elapsed time to impact would have been about three minutes. That leaves ten minutes for the flight from Watertown to the turn. The straight-line distance from Watertown to the turn is eighty-two miles, the speed required to complete in ten minutes is about 480 mph. Given the lack of precision regarding the time of the crash ("approximately 2:10 p.m.") the estimates of speed for the two segments of the flight are close enough to be the same.

Bottomline, the flight path shown below is the most likely; "alternative flight paths" are the ones under consideration by the aircrew depending on resolution of avionics and/or radio problems.

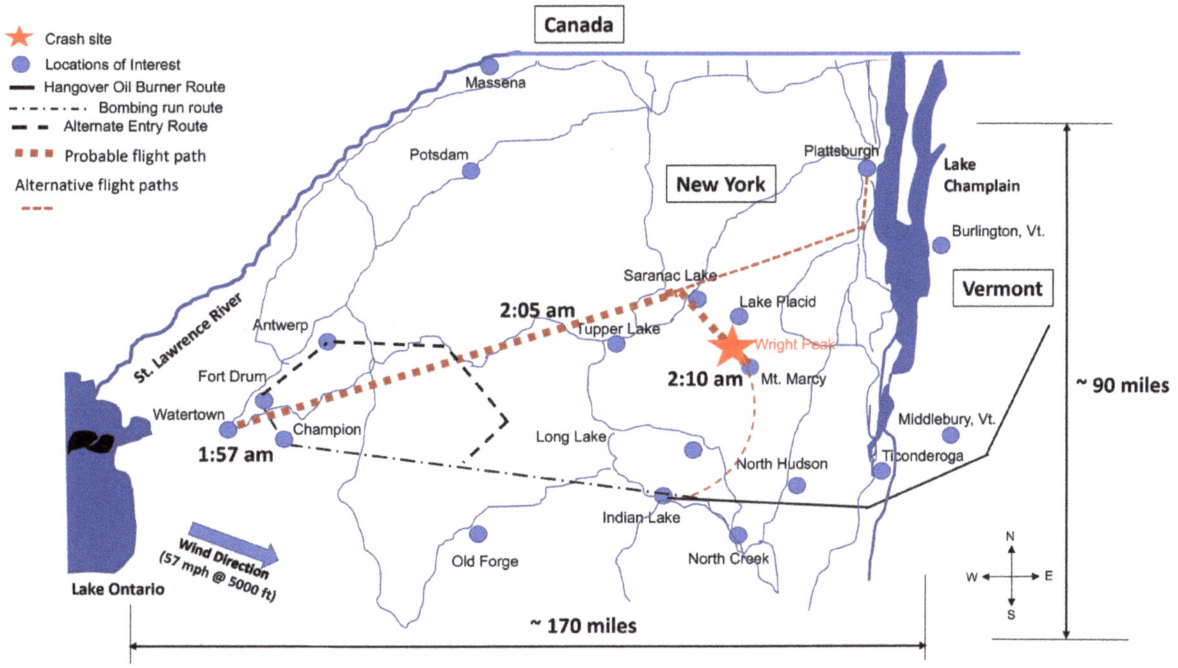

Image by Author.

5. Intermittent radio communications during the flight.

At 1:57 a.m. permission for immediate re-entry to the Oil Burner route was requested at that time the aircraft was "4 miles out from the Watertown VOR"; the Boston Center directed Pete 67 to contact Watertown. No contact was made [with Watertown][23]—and no reason given—leaving one to suspect the aircraft HF radio was experiencing intermittent failure.

Shortly after the 2:05 a.m. contact with Plattsburgh Metro, the aircraft banked into an approximate 70-degree turn on a course toward the mountains that would intersect the Hangover route east of Indian Lake. It would be expected—if the radio were operating—that the navigator would contact Watertown at that point to confirm the intent for a low altitude run. There was no contact. No further contacts were made to any entity, again leading one to suspect the radio was inoperable.

6. Deviation from the alternate entry route.

That the "Oilburner Hangover alternate entry, as published, did not furnish the crew commander with radio navigational aids to accurately monitor aircraft position during penetration"[24] is listed as a contributing cause.

The crux of the issue appears to be that alternate entry instructions as contained in the *Airman's Guide* [25] with an effective date of January 14,1962, for example, "Alternate Entry—Aircraft will enter at 43° 57' N, 76° 04' W (Watertown, New York VOR) at flight level 290 (29,000 feet); start descent, cross 44° 03' N, 75° 53' at flight level 250 (25,000 feet) direct (to) 44° 16' N 75° 50' W..." pertain to an aircraft flying over the Watertown VOR at 29,000 feet (not a much lower altitude) and descending to 5,000 feet in the vicinity of Eagle Bay, twenty-five miles west of Indian Lake. Further, specification of altitudes for descent in terms of latitude and longitude probably are not of use to the aircraft until converted to VOR radial beacon directions and distances. Presumably, this would have been done by air traffic control at Watertown in a similar manner to the ill-fated Ka'ala Mountain crash—but did not happen.

7. Re-entry Point Altitude Specification.

Based on the recollection of a navigator familiar with the Hangover route, altitudes were 1,000 feet above the highest terrain twenty-five miles to either side of each leg.[26] At the location of the turn, the aircraft was about twelve miles removed from the northern extent of the "safety zone," while Mt. Marcy appears to be barely displaced, if at all, and the 4,924-foot summit of Skylight is quite possibly within the twenty-five-mile span. *Ample reason to question the altitude specification of 5,000 feet for the entry point—rather than 5,924—or in round numbers, 6,000 feet.*

8. Terrain Avoidance Radar (TAR):

One could question if ground monitoring radar for warning of obstacles (TAR), now commonplace, in addition to radar altimetry capability, was aboard. An article written by a B-47 navigator states that Terrain Avoidance Radar was in the distant future and suggests that the radar aboard was just a position indicator.[27]

9. Location of the turn toward southeast:

The timing of the turn was very unfortunate; the figure below is a close-up view of the probable flight path in the vicinity of Wright Peak in red and several safe alternatives in green, like gaps in an irregular picket fence. One is tempted to believe the intention of the Pete 67 aircrew was to exit the High Peaks region along one of the "safe alternatives" paths in the southwest direction toward Indian Lake and the bombing run.

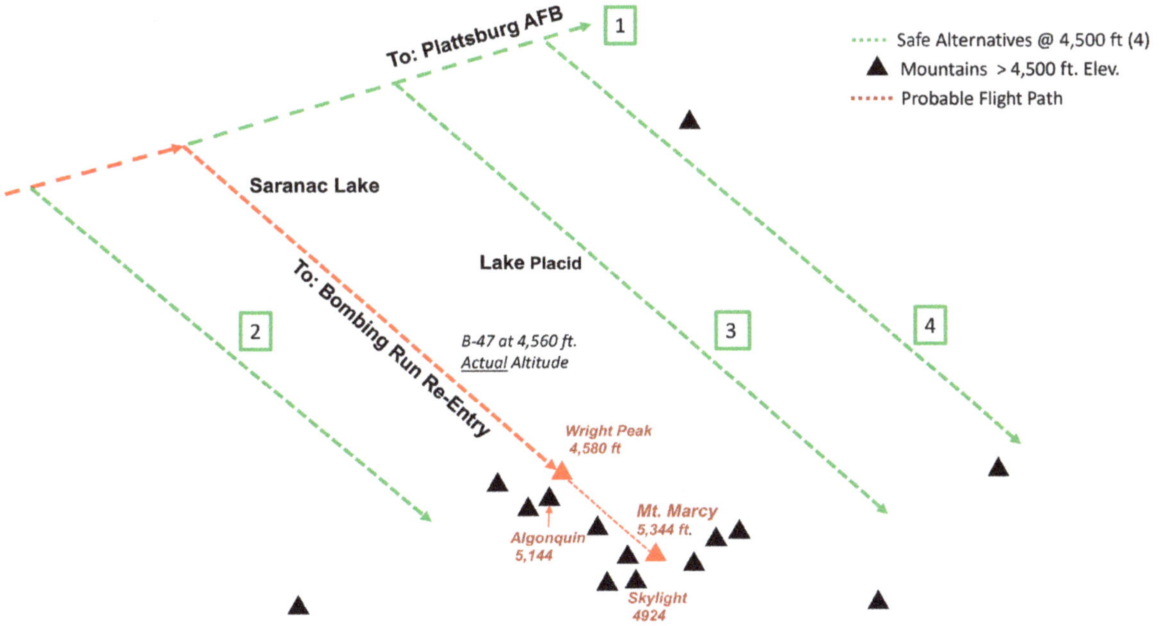

Image by Author.

Five to ten miles either way—or much less with smaller margins of safety—relative to the location of the fateful turn would have resulted in a safe exit from the mountainous region at 4,560 feet altitude. And while that may seem like a significant error, in an aircraft traveling at over 400 mph it is about a minute. Alternately, just staying on course toward Plattsburgh Air Force Base and delaying the turn to the south until out of the High Peaks region would have avoided a Controlled Flight into Terrain.

Finally, looking at the above diagram very closely, the flight path and its extension to the south-east, completely by chance, took the aircraft in close proximity to the only mountains in the range—Algonquin, Marcy, Skylight, and Haystack—close to or slightly exceeding 5,000 feet. *At an actual, not indicated, 5,000 feet flight altitude, any other path through the High Peaks would have been successful.* The crew was heartbreakingly close to a safe return.

PUTTING ALL THE PIECES OF THE PUZZLE TOGETHER—HOW DID IT HAPPEN?

A question of critical interest and importance, and one that has been on the mind of the daughter of Rodney Bloomgren, who conducted her own online research.[28] "No one," Michael Collins, a pilot acquaintance with experience in Adirondacks flying advised me, "will ever know for sure." But here is a speculative explanation that fits the facts:

After completing the second high altitude run, deciding to circle back for a low-level, "short look" pass and contacting the Boston FAA Air Traffic Control Center of their intent, as required when making en-route changes in flight plans under IFR conditions, difficulties were experienced with radio communications and possibly the entire avionics suite. This prevented contact with the Watertown Air Traffic Control as directed by Boston. At that point in time the navigator might have been aware that they had crossed the 70-degree, east-northeast, outbound radial signal from the Watertown VOR radio navigational aid, had a compass heading, and knew that maintaining that direction would lead them to Lake Champlain, south of Plattsburgh. So instead of attempting to follow the alternate entry route, they continued on a direct flight path toward Plattsburgh. By *dead reckoning*, if nothing else, they could proceed east-northeast and at the appropriate time descend through the cloud bank, visually locate the lake, and turn north toward Plattsburgh Air Force Base. Easier to say than do, and risky—as they were flying totally blind and with limited options—but very similar to the approach taken later in the search for survivors by the pilot of an L-19 Army observation plane.

However, still intent on salvaging the plan for a low-level run and, in any event needing radio navigation aids and radio communication for safe operation, Airman First Class Kenneth Jensen, the on-board observer, an electronics technician, went to work in an attempt to get their critical avionics systems back in operation. He was successful in restoring the systems (at the very least, the radio) to some semblance of working order—perhaps it was as simple as a loose ground connection—and at 2:10 a.m. the navigator contacted Plattsburgh Metro for recalibration of the pressure altimeter. It is important to note that while the information was in all likelihood transmitted by Plattsburgh Metro, there is no way to ascertain that it was accurately received and acknowledged given Pete 67 radio operational problems (similar to related circumstances of the Ka'ala Mountain crash, page 37).

With the altimeter systems recalibrated it would seem they were out of harm's way. Unfortunately, the calibration of the pressure altimeter, which is the standard means of monitoring altitude relative to sea level (and the basis for altitudes of mountain summits) was in error. The radar altimeter provides altitude above terrain directly below the aircraft, which is of little use in avoiding a mountainous region crash.

The next step was to notify Watertown ATC that they were descending, request instructions, and turn southeast to intercept the Oil Burner route east of the Indian Lake entry point. Contact with Watertown did not occur, probably due to continued intermittent radio malfunction. As the navigator repeatedly tried to make contact and the electronics technician worked to restore radio operation, the pilot guided the plane to an *altimeter-indicated* 5,000 feet altitude for low-level training run re-entry. Next, anticipating success in restoring radio communications, at a location based on *dead reckoning* by the navigator, he committed to intercepting the low-level run, banking the aircraft into a turn to the southeast over the lower-lying Saranac Lake area. It is reasonable to assume location of the turn was selected to avoid the highest mountains in the range; there are only two over 5,000 feet—Marcy and

Algonquin. While the path chosen would miss the summit of Algonquin by about a mile, it was directly in line with Mt. Marcy. That's the problem with dead reckoning—limited accuracy.

More importantly, the 440-feet pressure altimeter error meant that at an indicated 5,000 feet altitude, they were actually flying at 4,560 feet, not high enough to clear Wright Peak. Finally, Terrain Avoidance Radar, now in routine use, would come later and was not installed on Pete 67, so there was no warning of impending impact.

Continuing the effort to contact Watertown as they approached Wright Peak, which was not visible due to the cloud layer, severe turbulence (typical of mountain ranges) distracted the crew from further radio transmission and/or contributed to continued radio malfunction. This precluded any last-second, just-in-time corrections in route or altitude before the impact.

Taken altogether, the crash seems to have resulted from small and unfortunate deviations in timing, location, and altitude to a safe exit path in the mountainous region—complicated by severe turbulence, probable avionics and radio failures, and lack of navigation instructions for the descent to the low-level bombing run. From a navigation perspective, *everything that could go wrong went wrong.*

The basis in established facts supporting the foregoing, it is important to acknowledge, is largely contained in one section or another in the USAF Accident Report. It could easily have been a close call—but nonetheless, an accident avoided—rather than a crash. For want of a nail, a pilot acquaintance observed, they perished.[29] There are so many "if-only" factors, for example but not limited to: If only—

- the altimeter error had been plus-440 feet instead of minus,
- the turn location timing had been different by ten or more seconds either way,
- the turn angle had been 4 degrees greater or less,
- the radio had worked at least one more time, or not worked at all (!),
- the altitude for the alternate entry point to the run had been 1,000 feet higher.

One could add it was the outcome of the aircrew's decision to extend the mission to include a low-altitude run, an unfortunate result of their dedication and commitment to training. (And a more sympathetic way to characterize the accident cause than the Investigative Report statement: the "crew allowed the aircraft to deviate sufficiently from the published alternate entry.")

Shortly after the accident, a significant change was made to the Hangover route, as provided in the *Airman's Guide* dated April 24, 1962 and shown on the following page.[30] Effective May 6, 1962, the low-level bombing run entry-point altitude was increased from 5,000 to 6,000 feet, a change that arguably would have prevented the January 16, 1962 accident and was possibly an oversight when the original Hangover route was established.

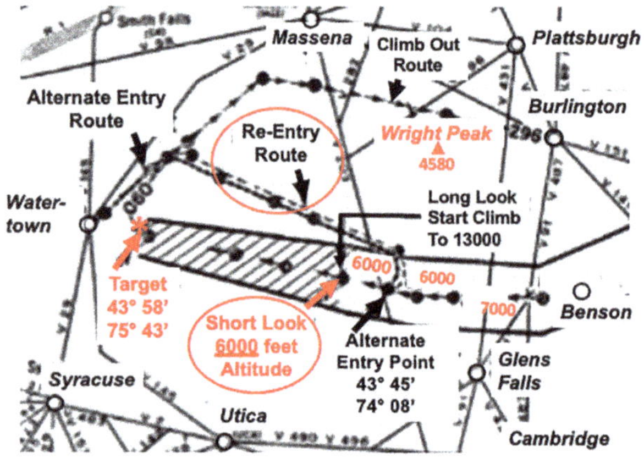

May 6, 1962 effective date. [30]

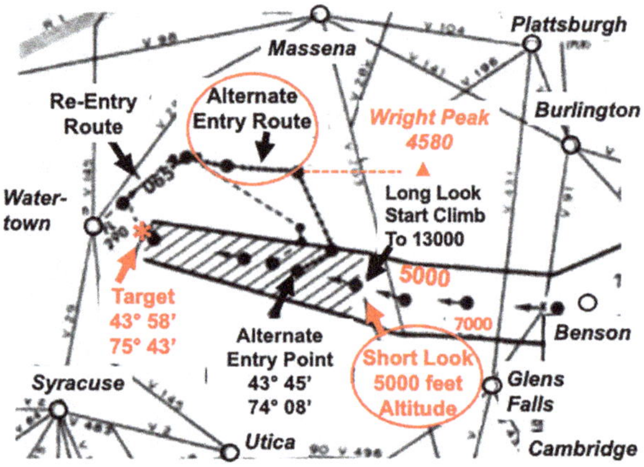

January 14, 1962 effective date. [31]

Images by Author based on FAA Airman's Guide.

Note the Short Look Entry altitude increase from 5000 to 6000 feet effective four months following the accident.

But, that wasn't the final step taken. Because altimeter correction values, reflecting local weather conditions could exceed -400 ft and, for example, the highest elevation in the High Peaks region (Mt. Marcy) is 5343 ft above sea level, only 657 ft less than the revised Short Look Entry altitude of 6000 ft, an additional step to provide increased safety margin was taken in the form of an altitude restriction on SAC aircraft.

In the words of Lt Col (Ret) Frank Baehre, former B-52H Co-pilot and Aircraft Commander and FB-111A Aircraft Commander and Instructor Pilot.:

> "Here's what I remember about the altitude correction. After the Wright Peak accident, although I don't know the exact timing, SAC added a restriction for that negative 400 ft combination of Pressure Altitude Variation (PAv) and "D" value. If the combination exceeded 400, SAC bombers (B-47s and B-52s) were prohibited for flying low level route training missions at night or in IMC (Instrument Meteorological Conditions). This restriction was in place when I went through B-52 training during the summer of 1973 and had been in place sometime before then. It required crews to obtain the most current PAv and D values for the entry, mid-point, and exit points of the low-level route they were scheduled to fly. We'd get the values from the Air Force weather shops as close to our route and entry times as we could, compute the combination number, and compare it to that [negative] 400. If any point exceeded that value, we couldn't enter the route unless we could see the ground and terrain, which we couldn't do if it was night or cloudy. By the time I got into the FB-111A with its Terrain Following Radar (TFR), the restriction no longer applied if the crew had enough experience and was qualified to use our TFR at night or IMC to climb us over hills, etc."[32]

NOTES, CHAPTER 6:

[1] R. D. White, "Crash on the Mountain," *Adirondack Life*, September/October 1983, 36–37, 50-52.

[2] Ibid., 52.

[3] *USAF Accident/Incident Report*, "Wright's Peak, MacIntyre Range, New York, Essex County, 10 NM South, Lake Placid, NY," February 12, 1962.

[4] Ibid., "Flying Experience," 7.

[5] Ibid., "Rated Non-Pilot Individual Flight Record," 24.

[6] "Local Flier's Plane Lost," *Jamestown Press-Journal*, January 17, 1962.

[7] *USAF Accident/Incident Report*, "Flying Experience," 7.

[8] Ibid., 10.

[9] Ibid., 12–13b.

[10] "B-47 Operations-36 Thoughts," B-47 Historical Website, B-47 Memories.

[11] USAF *Accident/Incident Report*, 2–3.

[12] Federal Aviation Agency, *Airman's Guide* 17 no. 1, (March 13, 1962): 17-Special.

[13] *USAF Accident/Incident Report*, "Findings, Primary Cause Factor," 4.

[14] R. D. White, "Crash on the Mountain," 52.

[15] *USAF Accident/Incident Report*, 3.

[16] "Debris of Downed B-47 Found," *Adirondack Daily Enterprise*, Monday, January 22, 1962, 1.

[17] *USAF Accident/Incident Report*, 41.

[18] Ibid., 42.

[19] R. D. White, "Crash on the Mountain," 52.

[20] *USAF Accident/Incident Report*, 42.

[21] Mike Hendricks, "Remnants of '62 Crash Litter Peak," *Associated Press*, October 8, 1989, *Plattsburgh Press-Republican*, 1, 11.

[22] William F Meader, "Crash Story Clarified", (letter to the editor), *Plattsburgh Press-Republican*, October 21, 1989, 4.

[23] *USAF Accident/Incident Report*, 3.

[24] Ibid.

[25] *Airman's Guide* 17, no. 1, 17-Special.

[26] Sigmund Alexander, "Memories of a Navigator", www.B-47.com/wpcontent/uploads/2012/03/memories.pdf.

[27] Walter W. Woodruff, "A Nav Heritage: The B-47," *The Navigator* 33, no. 3, Fall 1986, 17.

[28] Chris Knight, "Fifty Years later, pilot's family visits Wright Peak Crash Remains," *North Country Public Radio*, June 15, 2012, Fifty years later, pilot's family visits Wright Peak crash remains | NCPR News (northcountrypublicradio.org).

[29] Michael C. Collins, in communication with the Author, November 23, 2021.

[30] *Airman's Guide* 17, no. 4, Federal Aviation Agency (April 24, 1962): 12-Special.

[31] *Airman's Guide* 17, no. 1, 17-Special.

[32] Frank Baehre, in communication with the author, November 21, 2023

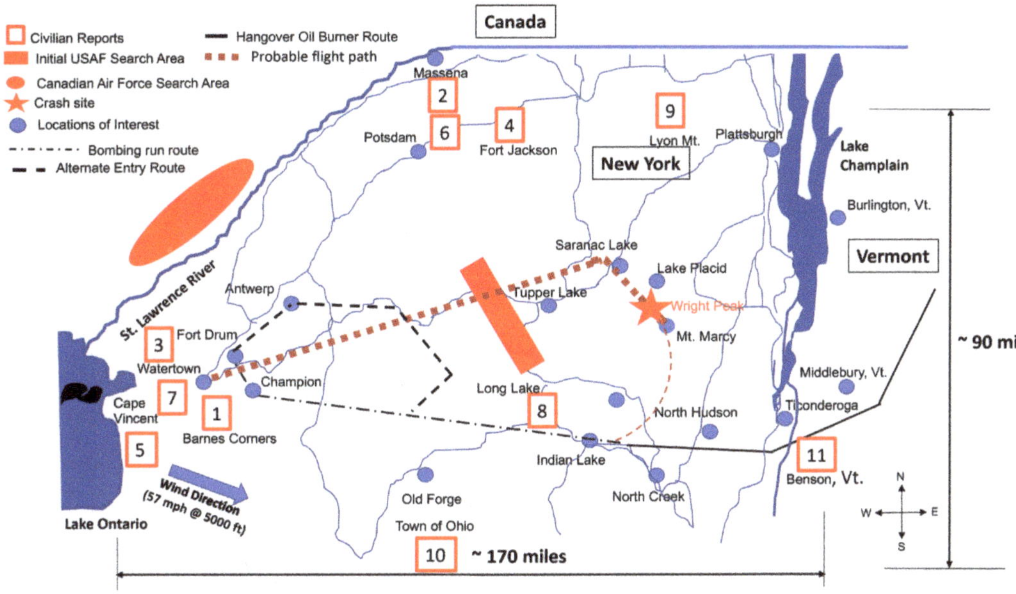

CHAPTER 7

THE FRANTIC SEARCH FOR THE PLANE AND SURVIVORS

While the USAF Accident Report does not explicitly describe the full route for the ill-fated flight, the initial search area coincides with a location spanning the probable route shown.

As reported in the Jamestown Post-Journal, a widespread search for the downed aircraft started on January 16, with Air Force and civilian planes "scouring the woodlands from the city of Plattsburgh to the Great Lakes. . . . [The B-47 had been] "due back at Plattsburgh Air Force Base at 7:00 a.m., with enough fuel to stay in flight until 8:30 a.m. Each member of the crew had a survival kit containing food, waterproof matches, and other necessities needed to sustain life in a remote area."[1]

According to an *Adirondack Life* historical account, "Troop B headquarters of the New York State Police in Malone issued a request that anyone who had seen or heard anything the previous night should report it immediately to the proper authorities."[2] Subsequent reports of unusual sights and sounds included:

Top: Image by Author.

1. An object resembling a fuselage near Barnes Corners that turned out to be a downed tree trunk.[3]
2. A flare in the sky near Massena and a possible fuselage sighting. A ground search was initiated and then abandoned; the police decided the report was in error.[4]
3. The same as item 2 above, but near Watertown.[5]
4. Flares in the sky near Fort Jackson. State Troopers investigated and found nothing.[6]
5. A whining sound of an aircraft headed southwest toward Lake Ontario heard by residents in Cape Vincent and Rosiere.[7]
6. A jet sighted heading southwest thirty miles south of Massena that exploded in a ball of flames.[8]
7. A predawn explosion preceded by the sound of a low-flying plane that awakened a woman near Watertown and jarred her home. Air Force planes repeatedly scanned the farmland south of Watertown but failed to find evidence.[9]
8. A very low-flying jet heard south of Long Lake at 2:30 a.m.[10]
9. A cloud of smoke in the Lyon Mountain area near Dannemora.[11]
10. A cloud of smoke observed in the Town of Ohio, Herkimer County, reported by a highway department employee.[12] An investigation was made by the State Police and a plane.
11. A large hole in the ice of a lake near Benson, Vermont. An Albany, New York, Civil Air Patrol pilot reported tracks on the ice of a lake and a large hole. Checkout of the report revealed the hole was caused by springs that fed the lake, and the tracks were likely made by skis.[13]

As shown in the diagram above the report locations were spread over a large area, and in the end none were productive.

There was speculation that the plane had plunged into the icy waters of Lake Ontario, but the Air Force determined that it had to be in the Cranberry/Long Lake area region[14]—again, *possibly* based on a ground radar observation of an image that suddenly disappeared or calculation of that being the location of the aircraft at the time of final radio contact. Hence, this was where the search was initially focused.

On Wednesday, January 17, in addition to teams of ground personnel, there were seven Air Force planes involved in the search, covering the area from Plattsburgh westward to Lake Ontario. Snow interrupted searches by planes, necessitating the use of helicopters. On Thursday, January 18, a C-54 Transport plane carrying a team trained for rescue missions arrived from Goose Bay, Labrador, Canada. A total of up to fifty Air Force and private planes searched an area of ten to fifteen thousand square miles across New York State and into Vermont, continuing the effort on Friday. The Royal Canadian Air Force, involved in the search of an area in Canada to the north of Watertown, discontinued their effort after four days—the explanation given that it was not one of great probability.[15]

While the Search was going on, the weather was miserably cold and windy. Temperatures in the Adirondacks ranged to 29 degrees below zero overnight. Reality began to replace optimism; a spokesman at the Plattsburgh Air Force Base said, "As time goes on, the chances for survival decrease rapidly."[16]

"On Sunday the 21st a National Guard pilot in one of five L-19 Cessna aka "Bird Dogs" single-engine observation planes from Fort Devens, Massachusetts temporarily based at Plattsburgh, spotted a wing and three [orange] parachutes around noon. The debris was strewn across the summit of Wright [Peak].... By afternoon New York State Department of Conservation Rangers, N.Y. State Troopers and other volunteers converged on Adirondack Loj, near Heart Lake 12 miles south of Lake Placid village."[17] Among the volunteers was 1st Lt. Richard Fletcher, US Army Corps of Engineers stationed at Plattsburgh Air Force Base.[18]

Douglas C-54 "Skymaster" Transport Plane. Photo by USAF, Wikimedia Commons.

Cessna L-19 "Bird Dog" observation airplane. Photo by US Army, Wikimedia Commons.

Richard had arrived at Plattsburgh in August 1960 to assist with the construction of Atlas missile silos, part of a shift in military strategy that would gradually diminish and eventually eliminate the B-47 fleet. An engineer by training, he was put in charge of overseeing the installation of the propellant loading system for the missile. A bachelor at that time—at first, he lived at the base quarters but eventually joined Air Force friends living off-base. One of his roommates and a close friend was Albert W. Kandetski Jr., bombardier/navigator on Pete 67.

1st Lt. Richard Fletcher, US Army Corps of Engineers–Plattsburgh Air Force Base, 1962. Photo by US Army. Source; Richard Fletcher.

On the morning of the aircraft's disappearance, the colonel he worked for informed Richard that it had not returned from a training flight. Using his training as an Army Airborne Ranger to support his case, he volunteered for the Air Force search and rescue mission with the colonel's blessing.

Richard has a clear recollection of the week it took to find the crash site and the arrival of an Army aerial search team from Fort Devens, Massachusetts. He introduced himself to the Army pilots, learned they were going to search a promising area of the mountains near Lake Placid, and joined them. As the search continued on Saturday, January 20, the weather started to close in. The planes were not equipped for instrument flying, and the one with Richard aboard might have become lost without his knowledge of the terrain. Following his instructions, the pilot took a 45-degree (northeast) heading from the search area toward Lake Champlain, dropping through a fortuitous break in the clouds where the Adirondack Northway (Interstate 87), then under construction, was visible. They followed it back to Plattsburgh and arrived safely.[19]

It is probable the crew of the ill-fated flight was using a similar tactic prior to a decision to re-enter the bombing run and turn southeast, which put the aircraft on a collision course with Wright Peak.

Sikorsky H-19 Chickasaw Helicopter. Photo by US Army, Wikimedia Commons.

On Sunday morning he received a summons from his commanding officer—the B-47 crash site had been located, and the search-and-rescue team wanted him to join them. Reporting to a colonel at the command post, he requested a compass, map, and radio for communication with the observation planes. Helicoptered on a US Army Sikorsky Chickasaw H-19 to the base of operations, buffeting winds made it impossible to drop him off at the summit. He was accompanied by a doctor and a reporter as they started on foot up the trail to Wright.

It was dark, snowing, and the wind was blowing. This was the first time that Richard had been on snowshoes. On the way up they met New York State Forest Rangers descending who had encountered 50-mph winds near the summit. Above the tree line it was impossible to stand, even with crampons. They decided to return to Adirondack Loj and make another attempt to reach the summit in the morning. Richard spent the night sleeping on the Loj floor.[20]

The next morning, in the midst of a storm Richard and the forest rangers endured a tough climb to the summit. Visibility was limited by blowing snow. The first "real sign of it [the aircraft] was the snow all saturated with JP4 jet fuel" said Jim Lord, Lake Placid Forest Ranger at the time, and "it took us quite a while before we actually found where they had struck."[21] There, all they were found small pieces of debris—non-metallic—a glove, a matt . . . no evidence of the aircraft. All hope for human survival was gone. Disheartened but convinced there was no opportunity to provide aid to his friend, Richard returned to the Loj alone. "Later that afternoon several sections of the downed B-47 were located."[22]

From the Loj, Richard was given a ride back to Plattsburgh Air Force Base by a state trooper. Upon return to the apartment, he was told that Albert Kandetski's father wanted to have dinner with him that night. Richard shaved, showered, put on a uniform, and met Albert Kandetski Sr. at the Officers' Club where they had a sad, emotional conversation over dinner. There, Mr. Kandetski gave Richard a book of Albert's as a remembrance.[23]

On Tuesday, January 23 a new center of operations was established at Marcy Dam. Continued severe weather at the summit forced cancelation of a base camp there. Enduring challenging conditions, a team of about fifty men, including a Boeing representative, picked their way through the debris at the crash site. The three parachutes spotted by the pilot of an observation plane were in a line on the southeast side of the mountain, open and partially destroyed by fire.[24] "It wasn't like anybody survived with them but they [two of the three] were still hooked to the bodies."[25] The remains of pilot Lieutenant Rodney D. Bloomgren and copilot 1st Lt. Melvin Spencer were recovered and returned to Plattsburgh by helicopter. The search was suspended on January 29 because of increasing snowfall and frigid temperatures. Navigator 1st Lt. Albert W. Kandetski's remains were recovered in May. The remains of Kenneth R. Jensen of the 380th Armament and Electronics Maintenance Group—*aboard as an observer with premonitions of disaster, but nevertheless filling in for another airman who was ill and taking his last flight to fulfill a training requirement*—were never found.[26]

As spring came and the snow retreated, more wreckage became visible. The point of impact is about fifty to one hundred yards north of the summit at a section of vertical rock ledge aligned perpendicular to the flight path and surrounded by enormous, fractured boulders. The aircraft failed to clear the obstacle by a vertical distance of thirty to forty feet—but if it had, the taller summit of and Mt. Marcy (5,344 feet elevation) loomed nearby, directly on the flight path.

NOTES, CHAPTER 7:

[1] *Jamestown Press-Journal*, January 17, 1962.

[2] R. D. White, "Crash on the Mountain," *Adirondack Life*, September/October 1983, 36. [3] Ibid., 37.

[4] *Jamestown Press-Journal*, January 18, 1962.

[5] Ibid.

[6] R. D. White, "Crash on the Mountain," 37.

[7] Ibid.

[8] Ibid.

[9] *Jamestown Press-Journal*, January 17, 1962.

[10] R. D. White, "Crash on the Mountain," 37.

[11] Ibid.

[12] *Jamestown Press-Journal*, January 19, 1962.

[13] R. D. White, "Crash on the Mountain," 37.

[14] Ibid, 36.

[15] *Jamestown Press-Journal*, January 20, 1962.

[16] Ibid.

[17] R. D. White, "Crash on the Mountain," 50.

[18] Richard Fletcher in communications with author, 6/17/21, 9/13/2021, 12/23/21, 1/30/22.

[19] Ibid.

[20] Ibid.

[21] Chris Knight, "Twisted Remains Mark Site of 1962 Mountaintop Plane Crash," *North Country Public Radio*, January 18, 2012, Twisted remains mark site of 1962 mountaintop plane crash | NCPR News (northcountrypublicradio.org)

[22] Ibid.

[23] Richard Fletcher in communications with author, 6/17/21, 9/13/2021, 12/23/21, 1/30/22.

[24] Paul Van Dyke, "Tragedy on Wright," *Adirondac* (magazine of the Adirondack Mountain Club), March–April 1962, 27, 29.

[25] Chris Knight, "Twisted Remains."

[26] R. D. White, "Crash on the Mountain," 52.

IN MEMORY OF
AIRCRAFT COMMANDER
1ST LT. RODNEY D. BLOOMGREN
COPILOT
1ST LT. MELVIN SPENCER
NAVIGATOR
1ST LT. ALBERT W. KANDETSKI
OBSERVER
A1C KENNETH R. JENSEN
A STRATEGIC AIR COMMAND
B-47 CREW KILLED HERE 16 JANUARY 1962
WHILE ON A MISSION PRESERVING
THE PEACE OF OUR NATION

CHAPTER 8

REMEMBRANCES AND AFTERMATH

During the summer of 1962 Albert Kandetski Sr. contacted Richard Fletcher to join him and family members of the crew on a climb of Wright.[1] The Air Force had made a memorial plaque and Mr. Kandetski asked for Richard's help in installing it somewhere on the mountain. On a summer day with reasonable weather for the three-and-a-half-mile climb, the party set out carrying the plaque and four evergreen trees, each with a crewmember's name tag, to be planted at a spot to be selected by Richard. Coming upon an opening in the forest to the left of the trail looking over the Adirondack mountains, the trees were planted, and the hike resumed. At the summit, stormy weather and the threat of nearby lightning did not deter Richard from mounting the fifteen- by twenty-inch bronze plaque on a vertical rockface close to the likely point of impact. The plaque lists the crewmembers' names and aircraft assignments followed by:

> *A Strategic Air Command B-47 crew killed here 16 January 1962 while on a mission preserving the peace of our nation.*

Top: Memorial Plaque—Wright Peak. © Nancie Battaglia 2021.

Another memorial, in a secluded forest area out of sight from the trail, was erected by the SAC 820th Combat Support Group. It consists of five separate bronze plaques, one for each of the crewmembers with name, rank, dates of birth and death; and below the group of four, a separate plaque with the inscription:

> *This grove of trees is dedicated to GOD in the memory of the young men who made the supreme sacrifice in the line of duty on Wrights Peak Jan 16, 1962 AD.* Followed by: *SAC 820th Combat Support Group.*

The plaques are mounted on a sturdy steel support frame and surrounded by American flags. In contrast to the weathered condition of the plaque at the summit, a great deal of care has been taken to keep the memorial looking fresh and presentable.

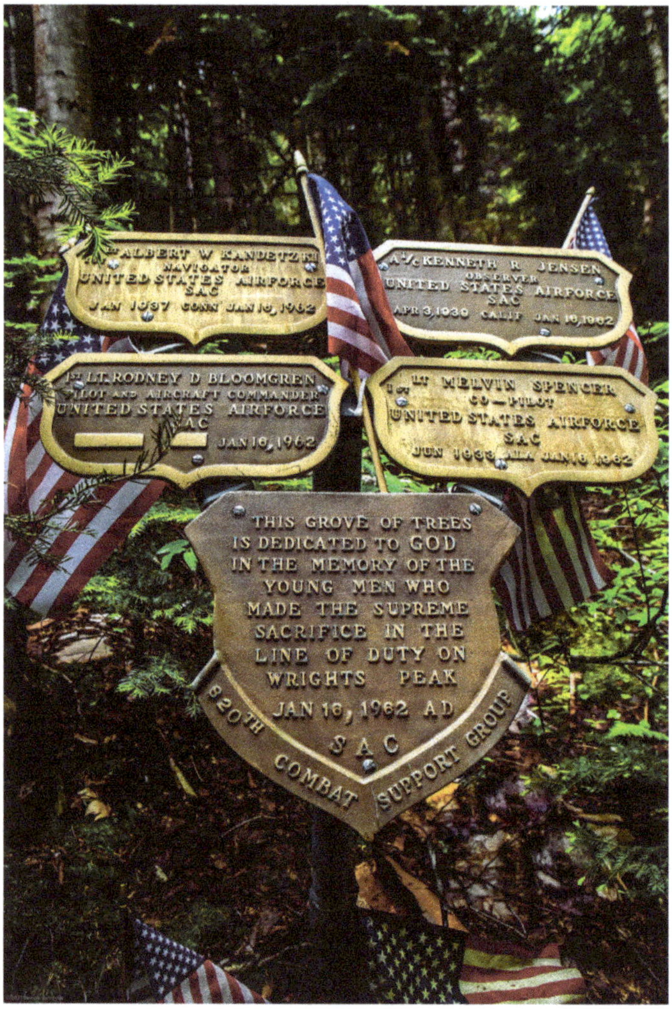

Memorial in the woods. © Nancie Battaglia 2021.

The sacrifice made by the aircrew and their loved ones is lasting and immeasurable.

1st Lt. Rodney D. Bloomgren, Pilot.
Photo courtesy of Cynthia Bloomgren Bosch

1st Lt. Melvin Spencer, Copilot.
Photo courtesy of University of Alabama.

1st Lt. Albert W. Kandetski, Bombardier/Navigator.
Photo courtesy of Hennepin County Library, Minnesota.

A1C Kenneth R. Jensen, Electronics Technician.
Photo Source: 1957 El Cajon Valley High School Yearbook

First Lieutenant Rodney D. Bloomgren, age twenty-six, left behind a wife, Connie Lou Crist Bloomgren; a daughter, Cynthia Sue (Bosch); a son, Steven Dennis; a sister, Jean Bloomgren; and a brother, Allen Bloomgren. He was the son of Harold W. and Edith Swanson Bloomgren of Jamestown, New York. He is buried at Sunset Hill Cemetery, Lakewood, New York.

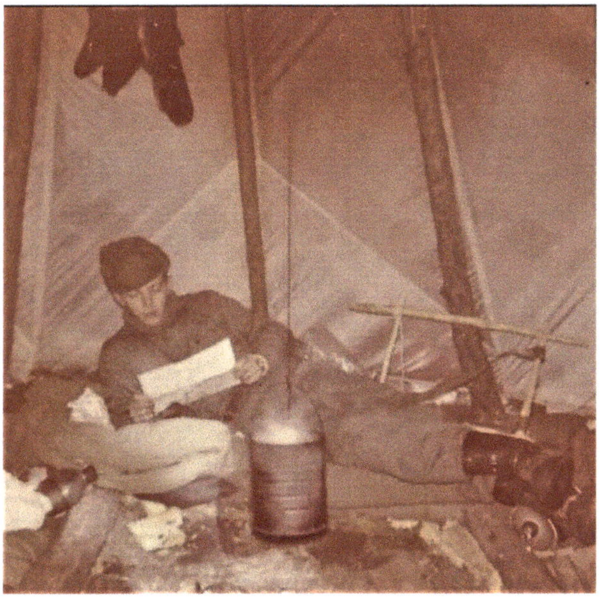

Rodney—resting while on a foreign mission.

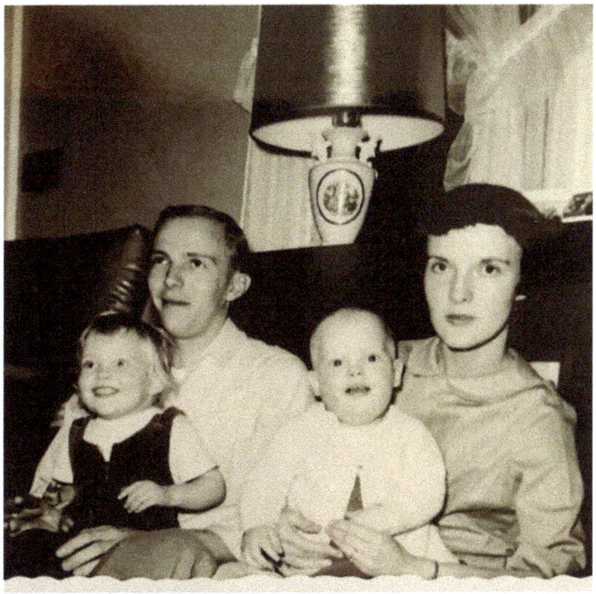

Cynthia, Rodney, Steven, and Connie Bloomgren.

Photos courtesy of Cynthia Bloomgren Bosch, 2021.

First Lieutenant Melvin Spencer, age twenty-eight, was survived by a wife, Lois Greuling Fleming; a daughter, Julia Spencer Fleming; and a sister, Mrs. Calvetta Ray. He was the son of Mr. and Mrs. Calvin Spencer of Tuscaloosa, Alabama. He is buried at Memorial Park, Tuscaloosa, Alabama.

First Lieutenant Albert W. Kandetski Jr., age twenty-five, left behind his parents, Mr. and Mrs. Albert W. Kandetski Sr. of Sunnyvale, California. He is buried at the Golden Gate National Cemetery, San Bruno, California.

Airman First Class Kenneth R. Jensen, age twenty-two, had a wife and daughter. He was the son of Anders R. and Ellen M. Jensen of El Cajon, California. A monument in his memory is located at Fort Rosecrans National Cemetery, San Diego, California.[2]

The summer after the crash there were more than the average number of visits to the summit, motivated by the scale and unusual nature of the tragedy as well as curiosity. Children at summer camps in the region who hiked there invariably picked up small pieces of the wreck as souvenirs.[3] Over the years, the amount of wreckage has decreased, most of that remaining either unidentifiable, embedded in ledge, or too heavy to carry out. Major parts still extant include a fragment of one of the engines.

"Hot Section" Engine Fragment. ©Nancie Battaglia 2021.

In addition, there are components of what appears to be the landing gear.

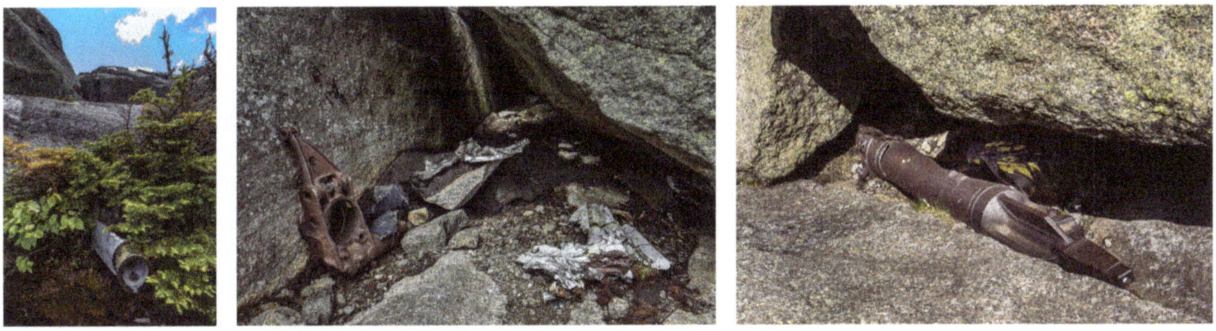

Landing Gear Components. ©*Nancie Battaglia 2021.*

While the enormous energy of the impact would be expected to shatter the aircraft, components that generally remain intact are engines, wings, and tail sections. The B-47 had six engines, and only a small fragment of one has been located, leading one to question whether a cleanup and recovery effort was carried out by the Air Force at the first opportunity—like the process reportedly followed after the B-47 crash at Emigrant Mountain, Idaho[4] and presumably also at Ka'ala Mountain O'ahu, Hawaii. A local newspaper[5] reported shortly after the crash that "a large piece of debris which could be part of the fuselage was spotted in a ravine" but its existence there is now questionable.

A simple calculation of probable trajectories for the 2,500-pound engines places them in the drainage area at the southeast base of the mountain, unless they were recovered.

After a period of time, the New York State Department of Conservation was informed by the Air Force that all material of interest had been collected and that what remained was available to the public. A high school teacher and several students subsequently located and removed the two tail machine guns left there; in due course they were informed that the Air Force wanted them back.[6]

A right-wing segment, approximately thirty-five feet long, was located some time ago near a slide on the southeast face of Wright.[7]

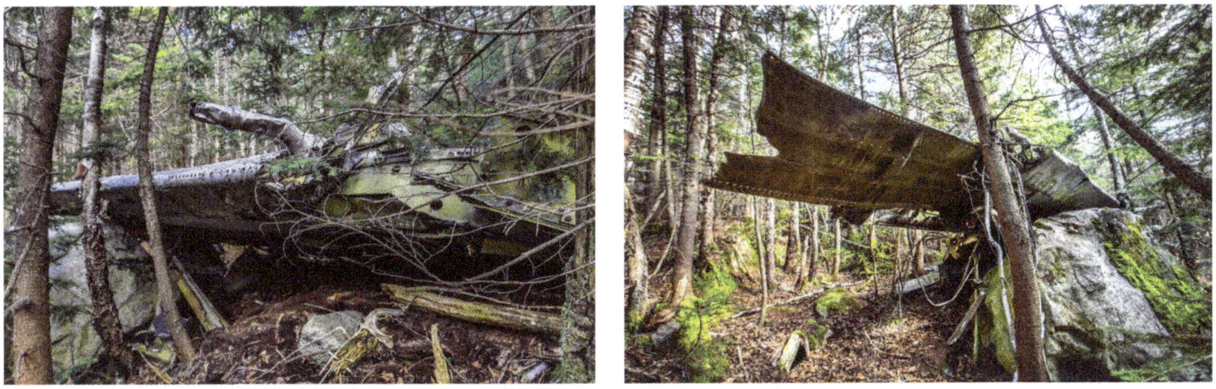

Right-wing segment views, southeast face of Wright Peak. ©*Nancie Battaglia 2021.*

The approach to the wing wreckage site requires bushwhacking in over rough terrain; and climbing out to the summit via one of the slides is "not for the faint of heart". Consequently, that piece of wreckage does not get many visits.

Southeast face of Wright Peak – Approximate Crash Site (1) and Right Wing Wreckage (2) Locations Indicated. © Nancie Battaglia 2022

Severely damaged by the impact, there is enough remaining to identify it as such. Interestingly, while this is the right wing, it is located on the left side of the acknowledged flight path, suggesting a complicated trajectory influenced by lift and wind forces after separation from the fuselage.

* * * * *

Descendants visited the crash site in June 2012, fifty years after the crash. They included Lt. Bloomgren's sister, Jeanne Morgenstern, daughter Cindy Bosch, and their husbands.

"Cindy Bosch was just two years old at the time of her father's death on Jan. 16, 1962. This was her first visit to the site of the crash."

"Jeanne Morgenstern was sixteen years old at the time." Of the days that went by with no sign of the plane, she said "I think that was the hardest part for our family, the period between when we knew the plane had gone down, and when nobody knew if they were dead or alive."[8]

"'Bosch said her mother, who died several years ago, never liked to talk about it. She has only learned some of the details in recent years, mostly through online research, and said it's something that has always been on her mind. 'I think about my father all the time, what could have been, and have crazy stories like why did the plane go down, what really happened? All that kind of stuff. We'll never know.'"[9]

After a strenuous hike of about 4 hours, they arrived at the location of the plaque near the summit and there the reality of the accident overtook them. They stayed there for forty-five minutes taking pictures and looking at debris from the crash, then descended, mostly in a steady rain.[2]

"Both Cindy Bosch and Jeanne Morgenstern said they hope people think about the fact that Rodney Bloomgren and his crew gave their lives in service to the country."[10]

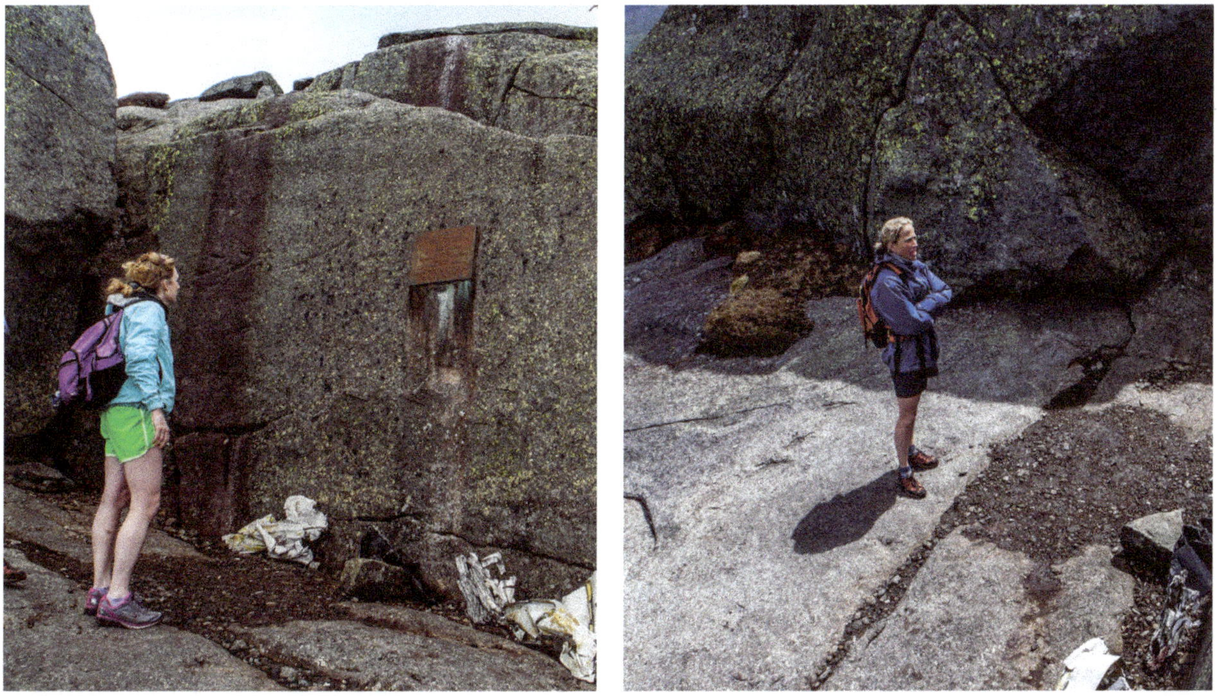

Hikers Paying Respects. ©Nancie Battaglia.

And they do; hikers routinely pay tribute to the heroes at the memorial, reflecting on the tragic accident.

NOTES, CHAPTER 8:

[1] Richard Fletcher in direct communications with author, 6/17/21, 9/13/2021, 12/23/21, 1/30/22.

[2] Ancestry.com, Library Version.

[3] Chris Knight, "Twisted Remains Mark Site of 1962 Mountaintop Plane Crash," *North Country Public Radio*, January 18, 2012, www.northcountrypublicradio.org/news/story/19141/20120118/twisted-remains-mark-site-of-1962-mountaintop-plane-crash.

[4] Michael Wright, "Debris remains on Emigrant Peak from 1962 bomber crash," *Bozeman Daily Chronicle*, August 28, 2016.

[5] "Remains of B-47 Crew Found; Hopes are Low," *Adirondack Daily Enterprise*, January 24, 1962.

[6] "Area Briefs—Machine Guns," *Adirondack Daily Enterprise*, June 15, 1962.

[7] Chris Knight, "Twisted Remains."

[8] Chris Knight, "Fifty years later, pilot's family visits Wright Peak crash remains," *North Country Public Radio*, June 15, 2012, Fifty years later, pilot's family visits Wright Peak crash remains | NCPR News (northcountrypublicradio.org).

[9] Ibid.

[10] Ibid.

CHAPTER 9

EPILOGUE AND CLOSURE

On a day in late July 2021, blessed with unusually favorable hiking weather—clear skies, low humidity, and 70-degree temperature—I drove to the trailhead at Heart Lake, and with an associate who had accomplished, through diligent effort, the objective of locating the memorial in the woods, hiked to the summit of Wright. The trail to Algonquin Mountain—steeper and rougher than I remember from previous trips—seemed to have an endless section of large rocks to step over, around, or on occasion, leap from one to the next. Prior to the junction with the trail to Wright there was steep ledge, which continued after the junction to the Wright summit. One can only imagine how strenuous that climb must have been, under adverse conditions, for the rescue team.

We visited the memorial in the woods and tried to find the clearing where the bower of trees had been planted. After sixty years, what had been a clearing then could easily be forest now, but one spot in particular held promise, and while the expectation of finding four trees with tags bearing the crewmembers' names was farfetched, confirmation will be pursued.

On that day there were several small groups of hikers on the trails, parents with children, the majority teenage, some reluctant to make the final steep climb; and in one case a small dog who behaved as if he really wanted to be somewhere else until the realization that he was at the summit put some spring back in his step. Close to the summit we encountered a trail crew member who was restoring one of the cairns that mark the trail. The trail is well marked and avoids areas of alpine vegetation, guiding hikers onto rock ledge. A summit steward greeted us at the top and was very pleasant and forthcoming about ongoing conservation efforts.

After resting for a brief period and taking in the dramatic views of the Adirondack High Peaks, we descended a short distance to the crash site, guided by a small handmade sign indicating the direction to the memorial plaque.

Sign directing hikers to plaque near point of impact. ©Nancie Battaglia 2021.

Memorial plaque. ©Nancie Battaglia 2021.

The vertical ledge where the plaque is secured in close proximity to the point of impact stands between two large, fractured boulders.

Within one hundred feet of the crash site rests the largest remaining piece of wreckage, the so-called "hot section" of one of six jet engines consisting of the single stage turbine that drives the jet's compressor, attached to a short section of the compressor drive shaft sheared off from the remainder by the force of impact, and the crumpled sheet metal remains of the combustor "cans" that fed hot gas to the turbine inlet and thence to the turbine exit to the jet exhaust.

Jet engine "hot section", point of impact in background. ©Nancie Battaglia 2021.

Jet engine turbine wheel with remaining blade. ©Nancie Battaglia 2021.

The longer compressor section and jet inlet were not found. One turbine blade, apparently rusted in place remains on the turbine wheel, bearing fresh "tool marks" suggesting that a souvenir collector used a hammer or rock attempting to dislodge it.

A few more unidentifiable pieces of sheet metal still litter the area near point of impact, and the several larger parts that appear to be part of the landing gear remain in place.

View of Mt. Marcy from the summit of Wright Peak. ©Nancie Battaglia 2021.

The views on that day were spectacular, including the one looking in the direction of the flight path toward Mt. Marcy and the other along the flight path from the northwest.

View from the summit of Wright Peak in the direction of the B-47 flight path. ©Nancie Battaglia 2021.

After paying our respects and with nothing left to view, we turned and started the trek back to the parking lot, clinging to handholds in the steep ledge regions and jouncing seemingly endlessly from rock to rock on the lower part of the trail until the descent was nearly over—and thinking again about how much harder it must have been to climb or descend on ice covered by four feet of snow blown by 50-mph wind.

* * * * *

The primary realization that comes to mind after research on the Cold War, nuclear deterrence, and the role of the B-47, is the airmen who defended our nation and engaged in a dangerous game of dominance aren't sufficiently recognized for their accomplishments. This is symbolically reflected in the weathered condition of the plaque at the summit of Wright Peak, and to some extent, action taken by the United States Congress in naming a ridge on Immigrant Mountain in Montana "B-47 Ridge". Both tributes are in the right direction but fall short when weighed against the sacrifices the men and their families made to preserve the peace.

Should there be a monument in Washington, DC in recognition of the Cold War Air Force heroes, their accomplishments, and sacrifices? They were the primary deterrent for nuclear war during the Cuban Missile Crisis.

One final thought—for all its capability and promise, the B-47 lacked reliability of systems necessary to make it a safe aircraft to fly. It is reasonable to assume that on most training missions there would be a system failure, perhaps more than one, that the aircrew would have to deal with—some serious, others of lesser importance. Ultimately, this led to a business-as-usual approach for operating the aircraft that accepted system failures as the normal course of events, and instead of aborting the mission, the crews took on additional challenges. In reality, the assignment was: complete the navigation and bombing practice parts of the training mission *and* deal with expected, but undefined (prior to the mission) problems of operating the aircraft. In this context, the tragedy of Wright Peak was the outcome of the critical timing of multiple systems' failures and weather-related burdens, combined with a route altitude definition oversight and a decision to extend the mission that overwhelmed the crew. They did their best in a very challenging situation to complete their mission and return home safely. Sometimes life is not fair. And freedom is not free.

ACKNOWLEDGMENTS AND SOURCES

This is my best attempt to identify and thank the people and acknowledge sources that contributed to this project.

Nancie Battaglia took many of the photographs in this book, located the memorial in the woods, and accompanied the author on a summit visit to complete on-site research. Tony Goodwin and Nancie Battaglia bushwhacked to the location of the right-wing wreckage near a steep Wright Peak slide for photographs and provided advice on locating period sources of information.

Wreckage of Wing on Wright Peak. ©Nancie Battaglia 2021.

Tony also reviewed the book for accuracy related to Adirondack subject matter.

A series of articles in the January,1962 issues of the *Jamestown Post-Journal* was very useful in understanding the series of attempted rescue events following the January 16, 1962 disappearance of Pete 67.

Richard Fletcher shared the story of his heroic effort to aid his friend, Albert Kandetski, his role in installing the memorial plaque at the Wright Peak summit and planting of memorial trees, in direct communications with the author. He also reviewed sections of chapters 7 and 8 and made corrections.

Michael Wright, Managing Editor, *Bozeman Daily Chronicle* gave permission to publish excerpts from a July 17, 2016 article on the Emigrant Peak B-47 Crash.

David Sommerstein, Director of News and Local Content, *North Country Public Radio*, gave permission to publish excerpts of June 15, 2012 article on the visit of Rodney Bloomgren's family to the site of the crash.

The first full, published account of the crash on Wright Peak known to this writer is found in the 1983 September/October issue of *Adirondack Life*. Not the easiest document to find, Mindaugus Jatulis, ADK 46er, was helpful in scanning and forwarding the article from his file.

The suggestion in the *Adirondack Life* article of detailed, unredacted information in the USAF Accident Report led to filing of a FOIA request, resulting in access to the full sixty-page report. Craig Fuller, AAIR Aviation Archaeological Investigation & Research, provided information on the path for submitting a FOIA request. José Gonzalez, FOIA/PA Program Manager-Kirtland AFB, New Mexico, was helpful in fulfilling the request on a timely basis.

The "USAF Accident Report" was invaluable in providing information leading up to the crash, including condition of the B-47 systems, flight path taken with timeline, radio communications, weather conditions, altimeter calibrations, and an assessment of causes for the crash.

The book *Boeing B-47 Stratojet—Strategic Air Command's Transitional Bomber* by C. Mike Habermehl and Robert S. Hopkins III, has a wealth of well-organized information on the B-47 program and is an essential source on such aspects as history of aircraft development, aircraft capabilities and limitations, and attrition records.

Mark Natola's book, *Boeing B-47 Stratojet—True Stories of the Cold War in the Air*, contains many first-person accounts of flying the B-47 to preserve the peace.

The *Stratojet Newsletter* formerly published by the B-47 Stratojet Association Inc., disbanded in 2018, and the Association's *B-47 Stratojet Historical Web Page*, are excellent sources of information from USAF B-47 pilots, copilots and bombardier/navigators on experiences in flying the B-47, its limitations, and accidents.

Warren Kozak's biography of General Curtis LeMay, *The Life and Wars of General Curtis LeMay*, is an excellent source of information on the contributions made by the General to the USAF Strategic Air Command's state of readiness during the Cold War.

Cythnia Bloomgren Bosch contributed insights on the life of her father—pilot of Pete 67—and family, along with photographs of the family prior to the time of the tragedy.

The University of Alabama provided a photo of copilot Melvin Spencer. Wichita State University gave permission to use a yearbook photo of Albert Kandetski, bombardier/navigator, as did the Library of Hennepin County, Minnesota.

Wikipedia was a useful online resource for overviews of jet engine development, with numerous footnotes leading to the original source material.

Retired USAF pilot Franklin G. Baehre of Plattsburgh, New York, provided useful information on the history of the Plattsburgh Air Force Base. Mr. Baehre is the curator of the Plattsburgh Air Force Base Museum.

Mr. Michael C. Collins, a retired Army aviator and pilot for New York State Police and ENCON and a past vice president of the Empire State Aerosciences Museum in Glenville, New York, reviewed Chapter 6—The Wright Peak Accident and provided useful insights and suggestions from the perspective of a pilot with experience in Adirondack-region flying.

Issues of the 1962 *Airman's Guide*, published by the Federal Aviation Agency, revealed an increase in practice bombing run entry altitude after the tragedy that would arguably would have prevented it.

Abigail Malangone, Archivist, John F. Kennedy Presidential Library, located a hard-to-find source of President Kennedy's observation regarding General Curtis LeMay.

Margie Amodeo, Union College Special Collections, provided an article from *The Adirondack* on the recovery mission following the tragedy.

Finally, I wish to thank Colin Rolfe for his skillful and thoughtful design of the interior and covers, and Dory Mayo for copyediting a manuscript of noteworthy complexity.

GLOSSARY OF ABBREVIATIONS AND TERMS

Ailerons – Hinged flaps extending along the trailing edge of the wings which are used by the pilot to bank the plane into a turn.

Alert Status – The basis for quick response to an enemy attack that provided twenty-four-hour readiness of one-third of SAC bombers for counterattack by aircraft already airborne and crews and aircraft on ground ready to take off within fifteen minutes, fully armed with nuclear weapons, accompanied by aerial tanker aircraft for refueling.

Avionics – The electronic systems on aircraft that include communications, radio navigation, radar and altimeters, and related display of information.

BRAC – The federal Base Realignment and Closure Commission, a bipartisan entity authorized by congress, operating within the Department of Defense, responsible for decisions on closing and reorganizing bases to improve efficiency and reduce cost while maintaining military strength and readiness for action.

CAT – Clear Air Turbulence. Sudden severe turbulence occurring in regions of clear sky that causes violent buffeting of aircraft.

CFIT – Controlled Flight into Terrain. An unintentional collision with terrain while an aircraft is under control.

Dead Reckoning – A method of navigation for estimating one's current or future position based on elapsed time, ground speed, and earlier known position.

ECM – Electronic Counter Measures. The use of electronic technology to jam and deceive enemy radars.

FAA – Federal Aviation Agency. Transportation Department agency charged with the administration and enforcement of civil aviation standards and regulations. It also works with US military organizations to control navigable airspace and ensure an effective air defense system.

FAA Air Traffic Control Center – A facility established to provide air traffic control service to aircraft operating on IFR flight plans within controlled airspace and principally during the en-route phase of flight.

FB-111A – The General Dynamics F-111 Aardvark. A retired supersonic, medium-range, multirole combat aircraft for ground attack, bombing, reconnaissance, and electronic countermeasures.

FOIA – Freedom of Information Act. Provides public access to all federal agency records except for those records (or portions of those records) that are protected from disclosure by exemptions or exclusions.

HF Radio – High Frequency Radio. Refers to the radios in the frequency band from 3.95–25.82 MHz used for aviation communication, government time stations, weather stations—which has a range of approximately 1,900 miles and does not require a line of sight between transmitter and receiver.

ICBM – Intercontinental Ballistic Missile. A land-based, nuclear-armed, ballistic missile with a range of several thousand miles.

IFR – Instrument Flight Rules. Rules that allow properly equipped aircraft to be flown under instrument in low- or no-visibility meteorological conditions.

Iron Curtain – A political boundary separating Western European countries from the Soviet bloc during the Cold War.

Long Look – Similar to Short Look in approach to the target continuing the climb to 18,000 feet, where the weapon is released in free fall to the target. See page 43.

NACA – National Advisory Committee for Aeronautics. A United States federal agency founded in 1915 to undertake, promote, and ensure continued growth of aeronautical research. Absorbed into NASA (National Aeronautics and Space Administration) in 1958.

NDRC – National Defense Research Committee. A government body in the United States created in 1940 for funding scientific research for national security purposes.

Oil Burner Routes – USAF training routes in several US States intended for navigation practice and simulated bombing attacks. See page 43.

Radio Navigational Aids – Ground-based navigational facilities that channel transmission of radio signals to aircraft receivers from ground-based navigational facilities generally in close proximity to airports. VOR systems are an example.

Reflex Program – Deployment of US-based B-47 wings to overseas bases in Spain, Turkey, and North Africa to enable B-47s to reach Soviet targets and return without refueling.

RBS – Radar Bomb Scoring is a military aviation training operation used to evaluate aircrews' effectiveness with simulated inert practice bomb drops near fixed or mobile radar sites. Radar is used to record the trajectory of the bomb.

SAC – Strategic Air Command. A United States Air Force organization responsible for Cold War command and control of land-based bomber aircraft and intercontinental ballistic missiles.

Short Look – A nuclear bomb delivery tactic involving low-altitude, high-speed approach to the target, followed by an abrupt climb to 5,000 feet and release of the weapon attached to a drogue chute. See page 42.

USAAF – United States Army Air Corps, predecessor to the US Air Force.

VFR – Visual Flight Conditions. Meteorological conditions when aircraft can be operated safely using vision alone. Does not apply in adverse weather such as clouds, heavy precipitation, low visibility.

VOR – Very high-frequency Omni-directional Range, a now obsolete short-range (200-mile) radio navigation system for aircraft, enabling aircraft with a receiving unit to determine its position and stay on course by receiving and interpreting radio signals transmitted from sites primarily at airports. The VOR site transmits radio "beacons" (think of beacons of light arranged like spokes on a wheel) in a radial pattern of 1-degree increments. The aircraft receiver interprets these in terms of compass directions (90, 180, 270, 360 are east, south, west, and north, 315 is northwest, etc.) and direction on a specific radial line relative to the source (in-bound, out-bound). Once locked into a specific directional beacon, the receiver is provided updates on alignment to maintain the aircraft direction in crosswinds or other reasons for "drift." Instantaneous distance to the source is also provided. With a set of written instructions describing required shifts from one radial to another for runway alignment and a specification of altitude versus distance to source (letdown schedule), a plane can be safely landed under low-visibility conditions.

INDEX

INDEX – PEOPLE

INDEX – PHOTOS

INDEX – DIAGRAMS

ABOUT THE AUTHOR

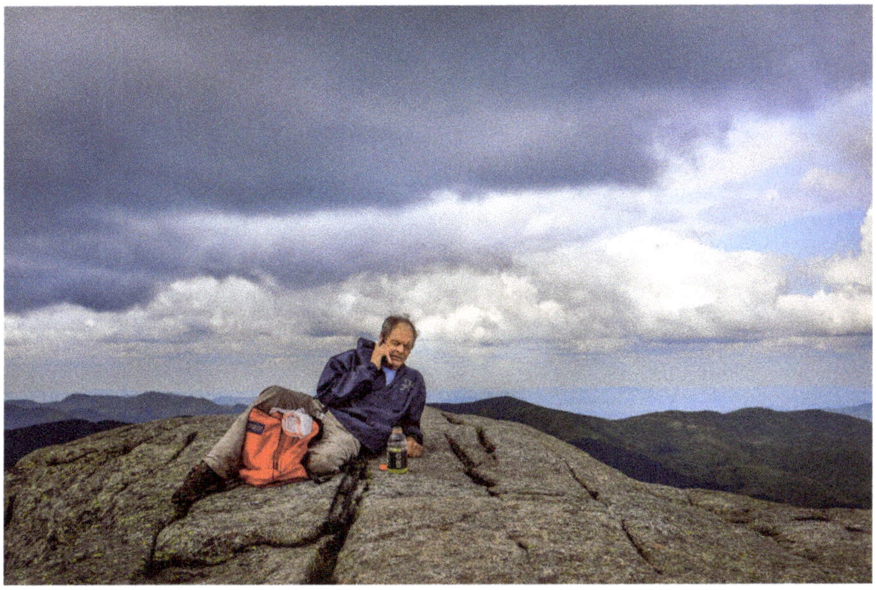

Author, Summit of Wright Peak ©Nancie Battaglia 2021.

Alan Maddaus is a turbomachinery consulting engineer with an interest in historical research and writing. He is the author of *The Prestons of East Street – The Story of a 19th-Century American Family* and has contributed to *Saratoga County Stories* prior to the research and writing of *Wright Peak Elegy*. His other interests include hiking and trail running, acoustic guitar, special-interest cars, and historical home restoration. He is a member of the ADK 46ers. He, his wife, Barbara, and rescued animal companions divide their time between homes in upstate New York and coastal Maine.